SOME DRAMATIC OPINIONS

SOME
DRAMATIC OPINIONS

BY

SYDNEY W. CARROLL

KENNIKAT PRESS, INC./PORT WASHINGTON, N. Y.

SOME DRAMATIC OPINIONS

First published 1923
Reissued 1968 by Kennikat Press

Library of Congress Catalog Card No: 68-8217
Manufactured in the United States of America

INTRODUCTION

My friend, Mr Sydney Carroll, is modest enough to imagine that he must be introduced to playgoers. I have tried to persuade him out of this misbelief by reminding him of his five lively years of service on the staff of the *Sunday Times*, but he persists in holding on to it. Now, it is very easy for a dramatic critic to be an immodest man, as I think I have abundantly proved during my career in that capacity, and Mr Carroll's reluctance to believe that his book needs any other recommendation than his signature to it, therefore denotes that he has a humility of character which is almost unnatural in anybody and is certainly unnatural in a dramatic critic. For we critics are a singular body of persons, whether male or female. Suddenly, and often unaccountably, we are invested with pontifical powers, and are permitted to pass judgment, adverse or complimentary, on the work of other people. No one has yet discovered how a dramatic critic becomes a dramatic critic. Sometimes, when I am at a concert, I ask myself how one becomes a player of the triangle or the cymbals. I cannot imagine any ambitious boy aspiring to be a player on these instruments, nor have I ever heard of a method by which one is taught how to play on them. Many times have I asked musicians to explain this mystery to me. " Does one," I ask, " receive a call to play the triangle ? Is it possible that some young man is chained to a counter when his heart longs for the day when he may bang the cymbals together ? " But no one has yet solved it for me. A similar mystery hangs over the head of the dramatic critic. Young gentlemen, lately down from a university, write to me, asking, " How can I get a job like yours ? " and immediately I am rendered incapable of answering them. Many little boys say to themselves, " When I grow up I shall be an actor." A larger number of little girls say to themselves, " When I grow up I shall be an actress." Some boys and more girls swear that they will grow up to be authors. But no little boy and no little girl ever says, " When I grow up I shall be a dramatic critic." How, then, does one come into this profession ? I give it up. I do not know. When I cast my mind back I cannot imagine how I came to be a dramatic critic, and I am certain that if Mr Carroll were put on oath he could not say how he became one. Clearly, one comes to this business with a taste for the theatre. All the little boys and girls who swore that they would go on the stage or become authors when they grew up, found, when the time of growing-up was over, that they were incapable of becoming actors or authors, so they satisfied their love of the theatre by becoming critics. All of us, I suppose, are critics because we could not be anything else.

And yet that cannot be entirely true, for some of us have been, and are, something else quite ably. Mr Carroll, for example, conducts an important business with great skill and success, and may be said to have done dramatic criticism entirely for amusement. Amusement! you exclaim in astonishment. Would anyone do this job for fun? you add incredulously. Well, yes, many people would, and, indeed, you ought not to do it for money if you would not be prepared, if necessary, to do it for fun. The best reason for doing anything is that you like doing it: the worst reason for doing anything is that you are paid to do it. I am sure that Mr Carroll enjoyed doing criticism, even if the people whom he criticised did not share his enjoyment; and I suspect that he left the staff of the *Sunday Times* with deep regret. He had made himself conspicuous in his corner of the paper, and no man likes to quit a place which he has made for himself. I am certain that most of his readers were sorry to part from his company.

Not that one always, or even often, agreed with him. For my part I flatly disagreed with many of his judgments. I think, for example, that his criticism of Miss Pauline Lord in Mr Eugene O'Neill's play, "Anna Christie," was written when he was not using his mind. I remember him coming to me, soon after the first performance of that play, and showing me a letter he had received from a theatre-manager congratulating him on his criticism of Miss Lord's performance. The theatre-manager agreed with every word that Mr Carroll had said about that remarkably fine actress. I was not impressed, for that theatre-manager was busily engaged in "starring" a pleasant young creature who, in my judgment, could not act at all. Mr Carroll certainly had his lapses, but then we all have our lapses, and anyhow, a man's capacity to interest us does not depend upon his capacity to make us agree with him. Dramatic criticism, like any other sort of criticism, is an expression of personal opinion ; and the more clearly the critic reveals the fact that his judgments are merely his opinions, the more interesting they become. The very fact that we do not agree with him may be the principal reason why we are interested in what he has to say.

In this book, there is an interesting speculation on the fate of Macbeth. Mr Carroll is convinced that Shakespeare intended Macbeth to be the victim of destiny; and he makes a number of quotations from the play to support his point, reinforcing them with the opinions of eminent persons who have discussed the theme. I do not share Mr Carroll's views on this point. Macbeth seems to be a doomed and destined man, but he has the right to make a choice. Even while he is deliberating on the murder of Duncan, he asserts that " we still have judgment here." He has

> no spur
> To prick the sides of my intent, but only
> Vaulting ambition.

When the Witches announce the increase of honours he is to receive, Banquo reminds him that these may not be the decisions of a beneficent deity, but the temptations of a maleficent one.

> And oftentimes to win us to our harm,
> The instruments of darkness tell us truths;
> Win us with honest trifles, to betray's
> In deepest consequence.

These honours that the Witches prophesy will come to him if he decides to do evil deeds, but he is not compelled to do them : he still has judgment here and can refuse ; and for a while he does refuse. The evil choice is definitely made only after he has suffered the chastisement of his wife's valorous tongue ; and even then, he still has time to hesitate and withdraw.

But one's disagreement with Mr Carroll does not prevent one from an intense interest in his opinion ; and what is true of his speculations on Macbeth is true of his opinions and speculations on other matters. He always wrote what he thought, even if it made him unpopular, and because he truly stated his thoughts our interest was excited.

The fact that he was dramatic critic of the *Sunday Times* when I was dramatic critic of the *Observer* seemed to make rivals of us. People used sometimes to say to me, " Your rival, Sydney Carroll, says so-and-so ! " and I daresay they went to him and said, " Your rival, Ervine, says so-and-so ! " I never understood why this assumption of rivalry between us was made. We certainly did not feel that we were rivals in any way whatsoever. We were, and remain, very good friends. I hope he read me as regularly as I read him. Whether he did or not, I do not know, but I do know that I was glad to be his friend, and to have him for mine. His industry and energy always astonished me. Not

only did he conduct a large business and write
dramatic criticism (an exhausting job in itself),
but he took a prominent part in the affairs of
the Critics' Circle, and was continually discovering
means of providing more work for his colleagues
to do. He was the originator of the competition
for Schools of Acting, and very heartily was he
cursed and damned by the rest of us for his
activity in that matter. We found ourselves
pledged to the improvement of acting by testing
the Schools in a competition ; and in a remarkably short space of time, Mr Carroll had
us sitting on committees and sub-committees
and conferences entirely against our will. In
the heat of the summer, Miss Hilda Trevelyan,
Mrs Searle, Mr Basil Dean, Mr Carroll, and
myself, sat through six performances of each of
three scenes from plays until we had found
winners for the prizes. The only member of
the band who got complete enjoyment from
the ordeal was Mr Carroll. He wanted that
competition arranged and he got it arranged.
There is no resisting him when he has set his
mind on a thing.

The career of Mr Carroll does, I think, prove
that a man becomes a dramatic critic because
he has a craving for the theatre which amounts
to a passion. Even Mr Walkley must have
some affection for it, although there never was

such a dissembler as Mr Walkley. The amount of money which a man receives for criticising plays is not sufficient to make him undergo the labour and torture of attending the theatre a hundred and fifty times a year. An incompetent pugilist receives more money for being knocked silly in fifteen seconds than a dramatic critic receives for the better part of ten years' servitude to the drama. Clearly, if Mr Carroll had wished to increase his fortune, he should have chosen to be a boxer rather than a dramatic critic. But he has this wild love of the theatre which has cast a permanent blight over the lives of many persons, and he could not do otherwise than take the job of criticising it when the job was offered to him. I have noticed that critics when they retire from their employment, continue to visit the play. They contract, with great difficulty, the habit of paying for seats, and the old war horses come to sniff the scent of the battle in the pretence that they have really come to jeer at the horses still in harness. Mr William Archer flits through the theatre so persistently that one half suspects him of wishing that "The Green Goddess" had been a failure so that he might still be writing about other men's plays. And very often I see Mr Carroll seated in a stall, with a sort of regretful look in his eyes. He sighs a great deal, and no doubt innocent persons imagine that the play distresses him, but those sighs are for a pen and some ink and his corner in the *Sunday Times*. This freedom he has taken from the bondage of criticism does not really please him. We are all like that. Once we have become the creature of the drama, we are held to her for ever, even when we contrive to break our chains, and I fully expect to hear some day that Mr Carroll has re-entered the Critics' Circle. There will be some consternation, no doubt, when he does so, and people now breathing in ease will begin to breathe hard and fast; but there will also be some pleasure. There are not so many good war-horses about that the absence of one can go unnoticed or its return be unwelcomed. And this particular war-horse happens to be a very good fellow who earned and kept the regard of his colleagues for the whole of the time that he was in their company. And now, ladies and gentlemen, he will speak for himself.

ST JOHN ERVINE

October 23, 1923.

CONTENTS

TO THE PLAYGOER

I WAS, once upon a time, a Dramatic Critic. Probably you have never heard of me. Probably you have never read a line of my criticisms, not even in the playhouse programmes—those theatrical scrap-books in which extracts from the great minds of the theatre usually find an ignoble but merited end.

I was only a Dramatic Critic for a short while. I held that position on *The Sunday Times* for five years—from June 1918 to June 1923. If a trifle violent in character, my offences were limited in extent. My Editor, a shrinking little man with an enormous blue pencil and a great idea of the value of restraint and sanity, kept me, with difficulty, from exhibiting greater ferocity and boorishness. If he had not done so, Heaven alone knows what difficulties I should have landed myself (and him) in by my writings. As it was, I am assured that they made his existence more or less tremulous. I can only plead by way of extenuation that my own sufferings in the theatre might have driven many a more highly strung writer into the madhouse.

I have refrained from repeating the criticisms on individual plays and players except in a few instances. The chapters consist principally of essays and contributions of a less ephemeral and transitory nature.

I cannot describe the relief that it is to me to be no longer compelled to state publicly my views upon actors and authors. My personal liberty is of greater consequence to me than criticism. I can now meet any actress, however indifferent her acting, with a smile and a fearless offer to shake her by the hand if she feels inclined to extend me such a courtesy. I am no longer under the necessity of crawling, a furtive slithering worm, pencil in hand, into one of Mr Cochran's cheap stalls at the back of a theatre pillar, or on the line of what the critics call " the death-draught." I now pay for my seats in 'the same way as you must do (when the piece is a success), and I can openly proclaim in the theatre my assent or disagreement with playgoers' verdicts.

In serving these newspaper articles up in a more durable exterior than they have had hitherto, I can only express the hope that they have not become cold or " hard-baked " in the interval. I have the time-honoured excuse of precedent to offer for their re-publication, together with the fact that I have been asked to reprint them in book form by many of my theatrical friends.

If some of the sentences I have written now seem a little out of date, or if my opinions have been contradicted by subsequent happenings, you, as a playgoer, will be able to make allowances for the alterations caused by time, and flatter me by attributing a few of the good results to my writings.

I dedicate this book not to you, but to " The Critics' Circle "—an interesting association of theatrical journalists in which I have had a special and official interest. You may not have heard of this Circle. It performs its duties silently and unobtrusively. It does not sit like King Arthur's knights, around a round table, but it comprises many elderly and forbidding old fogies who work tremendously hard at dramatic journalism for very little reward. Whilst I was among them they regarded me with affectionate pity and toleration. Each of them displayed towards me the attitude that he might have adopted towards a mutinous prodigal son whom he could never persuade to return. They contemplated my journalistic antics once a week and the behaviour of Mr St John Ervine and myself at the Council table with the same apprehensive look that they might have bestowed upon a keg of gunpowder and a lighted match in juxtaposition. I left them with the greatest regret, after having forged a band of harmony between them and the Theatrical Managers' Association. For me a strange accomplishment. I am most curious to know how it will work. I had thought of reviving the ancient comparison when referring to it of the lion lying down with the lamb, but I should not know which was which.

Opinions are worth while only when they stimulate us to think for ourselves. Mine are not intended for blind acceptance. I tender you these few ideas and observations in no spirit of dogmatism, but for what they are worth, only after assuring you, though I hope you need no such fortifying, of my absolute sincerity.

I am still one of you—a playgoer. Though I have given up my task of public criticism, I am still the slave of duty to my first, last, and only real love—the theatre. I always have been a devoted follower of the drama—I believe I always shall be.

SYDNEY W. CARROLL

SOME DRAMATIC OPINIONS

I

THE STAGE OF TO-DAY

NOTHING indicates so clearly and unmistakably the vitality of the British Drama as a revival of the ever-recurring arguments on the causes of its death. The British Drama is always either dying or dead. It always has been. It always will be. And when eminent political journalists and notorious theatrical managers, to say nothing of brilliant critics, hold inquests upon its unhappy corpse, it is time for actors, dramatic authors, playgoers, and such-like ignoramuses to reach the conclusion that the British Drama really and truly is more alive than it pretends to be.

Has there been any decay of the drama in the last decade? I doubt it. I do not dispute the obvious fact that there are, at the present time, too many foreign plays now running in London. Our stage is being overrun with foreign artists, many of whom run over with talent, others with exuberant energy and nothing else. Theatrical business, although remarkable in certain instances, is not entirely satisfactory, competition of all sorts is having a serious and detrimental effect upon the box offices in the aggregate, and the expense of running theatres has become prohibitive. But I maintain that the evil springs from too few theatres in the right positions and from exorbitant profit rentals.

We cannot expect a stage masterpiece to be produced every day in the week. We have no right to demand financial successes from more than one in ten, nor artistic successes from more than one in every hundred theatrical productions. If we expect a higher ratio we shall, of course, be disappointed. The good plays are in number just as many and as representative, the bad plays are no more and just as commercially successful as they always have been. The proportion of failures is no smaller and no larger than it is usually. If anything, it is a little less.

Shakespeare has been, and is to-day, the greatest force in the English language and the English character, but we can have too much

Shakespeare when it is the kind of Shakespeare sometimes served up in London and provincial playhouses and exalted as High Art. And it is a well-known fact that the more Shakespeare flourishes, the worse the lot of living playwrights.

The kind of drama, the kind of theatre that needs State encouragement, is the drama of our own times, the local theatre that will give employment to native dramatists, that will reflect our present civilisation or lack of it, and the artistic currents of the present generation that will record for us the life and manners of each section of our civilisation and every quarter of our land. The theatre must place beauty before eroticism and idealistic purpose in front of profit.

The cry of every management is that it cannot find plays, that the dramatic authors are either idle or incompetent. What is their justification for such an assertion? We have numbers of clever writers biding their time, but sick with hope deferred and manuscripts lost in stuffy drawers. I have frequently advised the Theatrical Managers' Association to provide its own experimental theatre and to pool resources in scenery, actors, etc. The

Managers could put up to auction amongst their own members the successes they discovered through this means. Has there been, or is there ever likely to be, any response to that suggestion ? I believe it is a practical one in spite of all internal rivalries and jealousies.

Many managers take playhouses for one play without the least idea of what they are going to fall back on in the event of its failure. They have no policy. Some of them have slender financial resources. But the reckless or improvident directors of stage enterprises have always been with us, and their percentage of failures is no greater to-day than it has always been. Certain youngsters in the game of dramatic journalism speak of the " commercial manager " as if he were responsible for the present alleged depression, and as if he were some new phenomenon created by the war, or some monstrous disease that never before had affected the play business. But what were our great actor-managers if not " commercial " ? They were much more business-like than many of the so-called " commercial managers " of to-day. Let us look backwards into 1913. It was a year of failures. Ignominy was the fate that attended many of the ventures. A play by Stanley Houghton could only run four nights. We had importations from France, from Germany, from America—the same glut of revivals, the same interest in " revues." The commercial backer may not have appeared before the curtain or on the scene as the dominant factor of the situation, but he was there exerting his power behind the scenes. He put his money on actors and actor-managers and playhouses, and backed them for a place.

We have seen the craze for spectacle denounced. But there is at the present time no craze for spectacle. In fact, there is, if anything, a dearth of spectacle. A good spectacle will draw the town just as a good play simply staged will always do. There is room in the theatre for all classes of entertainment. The play that appeals to the intelligent must not be given a monopoly. Spectacular productions make work for artisans and artists alike and must not be sneered at. In large playhouses pictorial splendour is not only advisable but necessary. It is idle to scoff at elaborate scenery, dresses, etc., on the stage. Each kind of play must have its own corner.

We shall not find a remedy for the ills that exist in simplicity. It may save expense, but economy in the theatre is sometimes synonymous with extravagance. It is absurd to say that you can kill Shakespeare with accessories. Nothing can kill Shakespeare. The actors have been trying to kill him for centuries. They have only made him more alive than ever. You cannot lessen his power with bad acting—excessive scenery will only make him seem so much greater than his covering. And if it comes to a weighing of the two evils, I had sooner see bad scenery than bad acting. I agree that sometimes we get both united. To say that Irving's wonderful settings to Shakespeare did not assist the imagination, did not give the production of Shakespeare distinction and nobility, is to talk random nonsense. Personally I find hanging cloth backgrounds dull except for certain of the tragedies, and I cannot imagine the public flocking in numbers to see them unless we can alter and improve considerably the calibre of all Shakespearean acting. Colonel Bell, who was associated with many of the late Sir Herbert Tree's Shakespearean productions, told me once that "Hamlet," when acted by that manager with full sets of scenery, always drew more money into the theatre than the same piece played with hanging curtains.

We must look for improvement in the present-day theatrical conditions to the actors of culture, refinement and proper education. They are there in the profession, but they need gearing up and cheering up. There are too many men directing affairs in the theatre who have no taste of their own, and who try to purchase it here, there and everywhere. The great play can only be discovered by the artist. The actor was first responsible for the theatre. It is to the actor that we must look for a vigorous assertion and continuance of its vitality.

II

A PLEA FOR THE BEAUTIFUL

THE modern theatre often reminds me of
Longfellow's rhyme for travellers :—

> Beware of the Raven of Zürich,
> 'Tis a bird of omen ill,
> With a noisy and an unclean nest,
> And a very, very long bill.

But the question arises : How far should an
age be held responsible for its stage, and how
far is the drama responsible for its own times ?

Ugliness may be said to be the presiding
vice of our nation to-day. Indeed, it is the
vice of the world. But what can we expect
from a world defiled and outraged ? Why
shall we blame dramatic authors or theatrical
managers for reflecting the chief crime of
the period ? I am constantly being told by
artists, musicians and writers that beauty has
small part in contemporaneous painting, sculp-
ture, music or literature. Why, then, should

the critic demand beauty from the modern
theatre ?

The principal defect of our modern drama
is undoubtedly its disregard of beauty, except
in a somewhat reckless display of the female
form divine. The interiors of our play-houses
were never architecturally distinguished by good
taste, but our stages were once adorned by
classic pieces, fine and beautiful plays finely
acted. Whither have these nobler concepts
vanished ? Occasionally a sublime thought
superbly executed graces the boards. More
frequently ugliness unrelieved and scorching
sears its forceful way through the whole field
of theatrical entertainment. Stage-land is not
without its Attilas, to whom dreariness is
Paradise. Were an author to deal to-day with
a beautiful idea in a beautiful way, no doubt
we should charge him with insipidity and
milkishness, and brand him as a sentimentalist.
It is our habit to incite playwrights by heavy
royalties and crowded theatres to rude, scandalous and debasing colluctation. The bedroom
may have been banished, but the Turkish bath
remains. Unpleasantness still seems the staple
product of the dramatist.

Whose then is the fault? And is it a fault? One will argue that the theatre is not a place for sucklings, that it was meant to deal with life with its grim and horrible passions, its fierce undercurrents of tragedy or melancholy, to touch on its varying moods, sombre as well as glad. Another will make a plea for the play that is an anodyne, and talk interminably of recreation, whilst a third flaunts indecent and unpalatable stuff with no excuse upon his lips save that of unblushing commercialism. Absurdity or conventionality in plays may be forgiven. The improper is generally arguable, but why such a wholesale contempt for the beautiful? Our modern playwrights are clever, some of them over-clever. They show powers of observation, characterisation, humour, wit and philosophy. Most of them can write snappy dialogue and bristle with smartness, but how seldom could we truthfully describe their work as inspiring, purposeful and beautiful. The perfect play we have no right to ask for. Such a play would have no excess, no defect. Nor can an ideal production be looked for. The ideal producer allows to character, dramatic effect, colour, fancy, humour, regularity, melody,

scene and sequence, each its just due and not
a whit more. Extravagance of idea and in
execution is as distasteful to the true lover
of art as parsimony to the spendthrift.

We need a revival of the Greek spirit. At the
back of this failure to give its beauty its proper
share is lack of courage. It was Ruskin, I think,
who said that Greek art was never frightened
at anything. That was why it was so beautiful.
Managers to-day have so much to terrify them,
heavy expenses, salaries, authors' fees, rents,
taxation, competition by the cinemas, etc., that
they may be pardoned for losing courage. It
is not possible for anyone but a gambler to
capture beauty under so many handicaps.

In some cases we find a tendency to substitute
realism. The realistic is interesting, and there
may be a certain rough and rugged charm in
actuality. There may even be beauty in the
rightness of it. But how often in the theatre
does the realistic mean the simply sordid, the
squalid, mean, and miserable without a gleam
of sunlight, the seduction of some poor girl,
the ruin of a simple home ?

I wonder that managers do not put in the
forefront of their programme more often than

they do the ideal of beauty. It must be such a
satisfying thought to be identified with something whose loveliness increases and never passes
into nothingness. It should be easy enough for
them to achieve the beautiful in a production of
Shakespeare. He helps them so. Latterly the
only real glimpse of beauty we have had on our
stage has been through Shakespeare. What
managers must look for is a sense of beauty in
the modern writer and the ability to interpret
the beautiful on the part of authors, actors, and
producers. Life for most of us seems terribly
dull. It means a routine, monotonous and drab.
Yet the people in the mass have never had more
leisure. The working classes have never had
more money to spend or more time in which to
spend it. To attract people to our theatres we
require something more than cleverness, smartness, trickiness and the power of entertaining ;
we need ideals. The theatre must have a great
purpose, and that purpose must be to show us
all sides of life, the fine as well as the shameful,
the exquisite as well as the coarse, the beautiful
as well as the ugly. It must help us in our
difficulties. It must stimulate us in our efforts ;
it must fill our souls with joy. If it does not do

these things, it is a mere pander, a base and
sycophantic snapper-up of trifles in return for a
smile, a male courtesan.

Consider the defective enunciation of most of
our players. One does not ask for oratory, for
elocution *in excelsis*, but think what little
attention is paid to the beauty of the spoken
word, the charm of clear diction and properly
modulated phrase and correct inflection. One
of the reasons for our modern incoherence in
ordinary life, our inability to make ourselves
understood in plain speech, is that pulpit,
platform and stage have each and all lost the
art of speaking. The stage used to be the great
preservative of public speech. There is no
instrument so thrilling as the human voice, no
vehicle of sound more wonderful in its variety
and possibilities. Yet in our theatres to-day
the voice is mostly an instrument of torture.

Consider the beauty of movement, the elegance
and dignity possible in human gesture, the many
shades of meaning so wonderfully conveyable by
a turn of the shoulder. Yet how many actresses
waddle, stride, stalk, or stumble like so many
paralysed ducklings out for their first parade?
Consider the beauty of the well-written poetic

or even the romantic drama. How long have
we waited for an English poet to write a play for
the stage ?   How long shall we continue to dally
with the discordant, the incongruous, and the
incompatible ?   When will harmony and unity
present themselves again ?

In making this appeal for beauty I am sensible
of the fact that we have some very beautiful
actresses.   The stage is crowded with professional
beauties, yet nevertheless is full of ugliness.
Beautiful women do not, however numerically
strong, make beautiful plays, though beautiful
frocks may go far towards making a woman
look beautiful.   The beautiful actress is mainly
engaged in showing her tragic inanity or fatal
fascination.

Where has the clean, wholesome and simple
play gone to ?   It is, perhaps, idle to look for it
when scarcely two managers can be said to have
definite policies of management.   Even so intelligent and spiritual a man as Mr J. B. Fagan
drifts from Shakespeare to Sheridan, from
Sheridan to Lennox Robinson, from Robinson
to Shaw, from Shaw to Philip Moeller, whilst
Mr C. B. Cochran, confessedly a showman, has
as many sides to his entrepreneurship as a

diamond has facets. He jumps with equal facility from " Afgar " to " The Man Who Came Back "—from Teddie Gerard and Alfred Lester to the Guitrys and Pavlova.

How can the theatre hope to make real artistic progress by such spasmodic, uncertain and irregular direction, however brilliant that direction may be ! Ought we not to go back to the old days when theatres were identified with a certain class of entertainment ? Each management would then have its own settled policy and would make an endeavour to adhere to that policy with the object of giving it a chance. We should be able to find comedy upon one stage, tragedy on another, farce on another, and so on. In this way the playgoer would cultivate a definite habit and taste for a certain theatre in the same way as he develops a habit for a news-paper, and instead of being dependent upon rumour and report to bring about a success, managers would have fixed clienteles to sample their wares.

Of course, it must be a great temptation to anyone conducting a theatre to show how versatile and all-embracing is their attitude of mind, but success is generally achieved by concentration upon a particular objective, and if only one of our managers would realise that a definite pursuit of beauty is an admirable ideal for a theatre, it would be an advantage not only to playgoers, but to the cause of the theatre.

Beauty is truth and truth beauty, that is all ye know
On earth, and all ye need to know.

III

ON DRAMATIC CRITICISM

WHAT are the functions of a dramatic critic?
Should they be those of a guide to theatrical
performances and performers? Should he act as
an index for playgoers, a signpost in stageland?
Must he write about all theatrical creations in
the same spirit, reckless of a sense of proportion
in regard to the standards of art? Must he
refrain from adverse criticism on a Shakespearean
performance because it is Shakespearean, whilst
he adopts an attitude of severity over some light
musical comedy or revue which, however trifling,
has the merit of making people laugh honest,
clean laughter? Is he in the Theatrical Propa-
ganda Department, or on the staff of the Highbrow League?

To my way of thinking the dramatic critic
has to consider only one thing. His aim must
be, if I may echo the opinion of a master critic,
the simple one, nothing more and nothing less

than that of chronicling his own impressions. The moment he starts writing for the public, for artists, or for his editor, he is a traitor to his profession. Dramatic critics do *not* exist to tell you whether a play is worth seeing or not. How can any one individual, whatever his capacity, however catholic in his views or widely sympathetic in his outlook, pretend to be an authority in so universal a sense ? Every man has his humour. What delights one irritates another. Preference has no boundaries except those we ourselves place upon it.

I cannot understand the attitude of mind of folk who are content to accept as final the judgment of others upon a play, a book, a picture, or a piece of musical composition. There are undoubtedly such people, but they deserve their fate. To such people criticism must of necessity act as crutches, but only as crutches, not as legs.

It may be argued that people have neither time, inclination, nor money to go and sample plays and acting for themselves, and that, therefore, they must be content to accept the judgment of critics whose business it is to report upon such matters.

Accepting this situation, the public is quick

to discover whether the judgment of a critic is
to be relied on or, what is of more public concern,
whether his opinion coincides with its own.
There are all classes of critics, just as there are
all classes of plays and all classes of players.
Each class has its value. Some critics refuse to
take the theatre seriously, treating it as a stand
upon which they can hang their caps of literary
skill, their umbrellas of histrionic research, and
their overcoats of general knowledge ; others
are satisfied to be mere reporters or storytellers,
to snap up and retail all the bright bits of
dialogue. There are several critics with a
passionate interest in their work, a regard for
the future of serious drama, and an earnest
desire for truth.

There is nothing so fallible as dramatic criticism,
mainly by reason of the peculiar and difficult
conditions under which it has to be produced.
A first-night audience is, to start off with, a
paralysing influence on judgment. Managers,
with the best possible intentions towards themselves and their authors, fill the house on first
nights with their friends and supporters, whose
lavish and ill-judged applause has a knack of
breaking in upon one's reflections. A crowd of

celebrities and notorieties in the stalls divert one's attention, the actors are in a state of nervous tension, and may or may not do justice to the author and their own capabilities. Oversights and mistakes are frequent.

A play is not brought into its proper being until author, actors and audience are all *en rapport*. An unacted play is a dead thing. An acted play is equally lifeless unless it is put before a live audience. The critic is generally haled on a first night to an improperly prepared, unfinished work. Surrounded by a mass of bias in the audience—he is expected to observe details in the production, to absorb the plot, consider the characters, the way they are acted, and to absorb and digest a series of momentary impressions in a retentive and analytical mind. He is seldom or never provided as he should be with a copy of the manuscript. He has as a rule to write his notice hurriedly, yet in the face of these obstacles people expect him to be a reliable guide as to what plays and actors are worth seeing. Obviously he cannot please all tastes. He can only be a guide to folk who see with eyes that are similar to his.

To suggest that a critic should defer his

judgment until after the first night is, I think, impracticable. There may be no second night. It is " on the night " that you must judge the actor or not at all. Criticism directed against the first night's performance may have lost all its point and savour with one repetition. The public must make its own deductions and allowances.

In view of the difficulties attending dramatic criticism, it is astonishing that our best critics produce work of such a high character as they undoubtedly do. Where English criticism is concerned one thing is beyond question, it is not open to corruption. It is usually a little too considerate of the feelings of actors, actresses, managers and playwrights, and written too much " between the lines." Personally I prefer to say exactly what I think. The Editor will never, and can never, allow his critic to write without check. But one thing is sure. Progress in art as in other things depends upon truth —candour. In my opinion, in the interests of all parties, it is better to be cruel and just than to be benevolently false. The critic, equally with the criticised, is liable to make mistakes. If he make too many he will inevitably find his level and properly be ignored.

IV

THE LATE SIR JOHN HARE

JOHN HARE was one of the finest actors of my time. He was a gentleman actor in every sense of the word in days when few actors were drawn from the ranks of "gentlemen." No young man ever made up as an old one with such popular approval or such obvious and elaborate trickiness. In his latter days no old man ever played old men with such sincerity, tenderness, feeling and charm. His incisiveness, his swift, electric manner, the dry constructiveness of his humour, carried him to triumph in almost every part he essayed, and his death raises once again a question that has never been satisfactorily answered—a question that is of the greatest importance to every member of his profession —viz., is acting a fine art?

The work of Sir John Hare as an actor provides an answer in the affirmative. There was in him not only artistic plasticity and finish of technique, but a joy in characterisation that placed him head and shoulders above the ordinary actor. His elocutionary skill was considerable, yet it never forced its attentions upon you. He gave you not only the externals of the character, the change of mien and manner, but he timed his movements and words so admirably that they appeared to come at the inevitable moment naturally and spontaneously, yet, although you would not detect it, in a studied and carefully calculated way. He could " listen " as well as any actor of my acquaintance. Although a little man, at moments he towered in a scene with the impressiveness of a giant. The comic spirit always lay at the back of his work. No one could so effectively combine dignity and impudence.

His career points the way to many a young actor eaten up with conceit of himself and satisfied with self-love and the flattery in which most actors live. It reminds us that there is no future for the merely competent actor. Our stage to-day needs the fine actor, the fine actress, just as much as it needs the fine playwright. There is no future for a playhouse filled with capable mediocrities.

The " fine art " of the theatre will alone restore its fortunes.

The actor, it must be remembered, holds all the other arts under his levy. He can claim the service of the painter, the poet, the musician. He subjects the playwright, the historian, the wig merchant, the electrician, the costumier, the mechanician and the scene-shifter to his moods and caprices. When he dies his art does not, as so many people think, and as so many writers have declared, die with him. It is handed down by tradition, by visual and spiritual inheritance, to others who have seen, loved and studied it. Forgetfulness of the actor on the part of the playgoer is more apparent than real. The great actor leaves his memories. Consciously or unconsciously, they assert themselves amongst his successors. Though he may go as he came, like a falling star in the sky, his light is reflected in the work of those who come after him.

Sir Henry Irving has been dead many years, but I can see still the influence of his work and individuality in the acting of many of our youngsters of to-day, just as Irving reminded others of his own forerunners in stage art.

Hare modelled himself upon Regnier. Others are pupils in the school of Hare. In judging acting as an art, we must remember that it is obscured by uneducated, unskilled, uncritical public opinion. It is confused even in critical circles by a carelessness, a good nature that defeats its own benevolence. It is handicapped by a lack of control not to be found in any other artistic calling. Anyone can call himself a judge of acting. Any scribbler can style himself a dramatic critic. Any tyro can label himself an actor and (without stoppage by the Actors' Association) can secure an engagement at a good salary and be paid whilst he is being taught the business. The worst type of acting frequently secures unstinted approbation from the ignorant. In the face of all these obstacles to clear thinking, how can we provide a satisfactory answer to the question—Is acting a fine art? We must, however, try to do so.

The Royal Academy of Dramatic Art appealed in the year 1921 to the London County Council to set aside the decision of the Registrar of Friendly Societies in refusing to certify the exemption of the Academy from the payment of rates under the Scientific Societies Act of

1843. The statute of 1843 was an Act to
exempt from County, Borough, Parochial, and
other local rates, land and buildings occupied
by Scientific or Literary Societies.

The question which the Appeal Committee
decided in effect was, " Is Acting a Fine Art ? "
and they decided in the negative. They did
not consider the question as to whether dramatic
composition was a fine art, but whether the
presentation of the drama by acting was a fine
art. The eminent counsel who argued the
appeal referred to so ancient an authority
as Cicero, quoted various judicial decisions in
support of the appeal, dealt with various
dictionary explanations of " fine arts," and
quoted from an article in the eleventh edition
of the " Encyclopædia Britannica," which he
described as a direct authority for the inclusion
of dramatic art amongst the fine arts. Yet,
despite all his eloquence, and notwithstanding
letters in support of the appeal from Professor
Gilbert Murray, Professor Bradley, Sir Sidney
Lee, Sir Walter Raleigh, Sir Arthur Quiller-
Couch, Sir Johnston Forbes-Robertson, and
others, the Committee decided that acting could
not be considered a fine art.

I did not, at the time of this obviously absurd decision, comment publicly upon it, because I was so profoundly disgusted by it that it left me practically speechless, but I have always held and hold that acting is one of the finest and most difficult of the arts. Of course, there are degrees of acting as there are degrees in the practice of such fine art as the London County Council admits into its privileged catalogue. I am not so rash as to wish to contend that all acting, no matter what its character, is entitled to respect. Acting that is merely an ebullition of physical energy, an exposition of acrobatic skill, or the power amusingly used of making grimaces or indulging in cross-talk and stupid pantomimic gestures is obviously disqualified from serious consideration. It may invite contempt.

The real art of acting calls for something higher and greater. It demands a sacrifice, a devotion to the calling, such as no other art demands. It demands in equal force the power of idealisation and the power to degrade. It calls for observation and imagery. In what other art is it necessary, for instance, to exhaust all one's passions, emotions, sensibilities and intellect to such an extraordinary degree as in acting ? The nervous tension, the combined strain upon physique, brain and soul upon every actor and actress exceeds that made upon any painter, sculptor, architect, poet, or brain worker in any other field.

The test of a fine art is whether it makes a demand upon one's imagination. Does acting ask from its followers the creative instinct, the impetus for which comes from the soul rather than the mind, the æsthetic instinct rather than the power of muscle ? If it does—it is a fine art. It is possible, of course, for an ignorant, inartistic person to act a part and to do it with a certain amount of success, but it is not possible to carry out any great conception in the theatre without a liberal endowment of the artistic nature.

Sir John Hare in his lifetime was, for the strength, the finesse, the clearness, the definite, delicate and outstanding clarity of his delineations compared to the celebrated French artist Meissonier. The comparison may not be just, but it serves to illustrate the relationship between the fine art of drawing or etching and the fine art of acting. The actor may

make his part a study in black and white.
The character he creates may be colourless,
steely, cold and intellectually finished, or it
may be a portrait as full of colour and rich tone
as a picture by Rubens. Who would venture
to deny that such pictures as Ellen Terry has
given us in her time of Portia, Olivia, and other
divinities of the drama are comparable in artistic
finish and beauty to the finest work of any
Royal Academician ?

The real trouble about the art of acting in
this country is that it is seldom taken seriously
either by the players or the public. Its
exponents are either extravagantly spoiled by
praise to which they are not entitled, or dis-
couraged by blame when the fault is not really
theirs. They are too often either personality
sellers or overproduced marionettes. They too
often, after the first fortnight, fool about on the
stage and " *kid their parts*." We who sit in
front of the orchestra know too little what part
the producer has played in moulding a particular
performance not altogether to our liking. The
picture we see may not represent the ideas of
the player himself at all. It may have been
painted to order, yet it can only be judged upon

the result, and not upon the processes that produced it. As for the public, they seldom analyse. They are pleased or displeased. That is all.

The use of the word " fine " in the phrase " fine arts " is intended, I take it, to exclude specifically any art which may, roughly speaking, form part of the material needs of our life. A carpenter may produce, for instance, a very fine chair, and the chair may be a really artistic bit of workmanship, but he is not entitled to claim that his work is a " fine art." Nor does the use of the mind by itself in connection with art entitle the user to describe his art as " fine." There is a great deal of poetry written (and poetry is one of the fine arts), but it could not be held that as nine-tenths of the poetry perpetrated is not real poetry at all, poetry, therefore, ceases to be one of the fine arts. Regarding acting as a craft, there are certain technical details connected with it that can be easily acquired. But what actor can give us spiritual and intellectual pleasure, awaken our feelings, move our emotions, and minister to our appreciation of beauty, unless he be a fine artist ?

Acting may be divided broadly into two

kinds—imitative and creative. Both kinds may interpret the author's meaning, and creative acting may and frequently does embrace the imitative; but the imitative by itself has no specific artistic value, hence the confusion in the mind of the average onlooker, who frequently mistakes very fine imitative work for work of true quality. It is not sufficient for an actor to put life into his author's character, be it a stage puppet or a well-drawn figure. It is not sufficient for him to vitalise the cold black and white of his text. His acting has to be endowed with that godlike gift of being able to endow a carcase with a soul.

The value of the actor who seeks to preserve beautiful, accurate speech must not be overlooked. One must hear English perfectly and clearly spoken to comprehend all its charm. The art of speaking blank verse correctly is a fine art. One admits, of course, that acting is as a rule transitory, impermanent. The effect created by a moment of fine acting may never be repeated. It may only live so long as the memory of those few people privileged to see it allows it to do so.

The cinema cannot preserve the actor's art,

for its secrets do not consist solely of movement, of expression, of light and shade. They include the exercise of human influence, the transmission of actuality from actor to audience, the mental, spiritual, physically magnetic contact that cannot be reached through the medium of photography. The telepathy that exists between a fine artist and his audience is inexplicable except in terms found only in the vocabulary of the fine arts. The death of such an artist as Sir John Hare makes us sensible of the value of the actor as an agent of culture, civilisation and humanity, be his calling an art, a profession, or a trade.

V

THE FULL MOON FASHION

I KNOW of no form of acting so irritating as the
acting that exhibits too great a consciousness
of itself and its merits. I have not, despite
a lifetime of theatre-going, brought myself
complacently to endure acting that betrays
an irrepressible knowledge of its perpetrator's
beauty, grace and charm. Too many of our
younger English actresses, talented, personable,
intelligent, have been taught, or unconsciously
have acquired, the habit of turning continuously
their faces, full moon fashion, direct upon their
audiences. They consider it is their duty to
register, for the onlooker's benefit, upon the dial
of their countenances every emotion and every
thought and to record each passing mood thereon
for all to see. They never behave on the stage
like people who, unconscious of spectators, take
part in an unwatched scene and who are oblivious
of footlights and audiences. They show a

palpable recognition of the watchful eye in front
and of the attentive ear. They seem to say to
the spectators all the time they are acting :
" Kindly note, gentles all, how smoothly I glide
across the boards, how amiable, how eloquent
and persuasive, how ornamental I am in this
particular part, how exquisitely I move my
hands and fingers. Watch, I pray you, this
gesture. Am I not an extraordinary, a delicate,
a sensitive piece of theatrical organism ? In me
you see a personality of the utmost distinction.
Please do not trouble to notice these poor
indifferent creatures who surround me, who
appear on the stage at the same time as I do.
They are but the trappings of my particular
regality. Be under no illusion, I am a wonderful
actress and the real object of your visit. Observe
me—my tenderness, fascination and elegance
entitle me to a position in your affections such
as no one else here can claim. I *am* the *she* who
counts."

Now every playgoer knows that these little
ladies are accomplished darlings and delightful
to look at. It is only a select minority that
realises that the actress, however marvellous,
is only part of the drama and not its whole.

All real actresses know that acting consists rather in being interested in other people upon the stage and upon the events and action of the drama, than in a too persistent and noticeable regard for one's own deportment, appearance and behaviour. The complete subordination of a performance to the purpose of the dramatist, makes that performance higher art and establishes effectually the reputation of the player for being an artist.

VI

SUNDAY THEATRE-GOING AND THE ENTERTAINMENT TAX

It is my view that the Entertainment Tax should be abolished. It may be argued that a dramatic critic has no cause to concern himself with the economic side of theatre-running. It may be held that the only things he should take into his calculations are dramatic results. I cannot agree. The critic, if he be genuinely interested in the welfare of the stage, should concern himself with everything connected with it. He must know its commercial as well as its artistic side. It is impossible for him to judge results unless he familiarises himself with all the details of theatre management back and front. He must be in a position to realise all the difficulties that hinder managers and producers in obtaining results on the stage.

The object of the Entertainment Tax is simple. It is intended to raise revenue. That the war

has to be paid for, and that revenue must be
found from somewhere is self-evident, indisputable. People who defend this tax say that
if it is taken off, another tax will only have to
be put on in its place, and that, therefore, it
might as well stop on. What careless reasoning!
A special class of the community is singled out
for taxation in order that the war shall be paid
for. Defenders of the tax say : Entertainment
is a luxury, and as such, it calls loudly for
taxation. They point, scornfully and scoffingly,
to the " huge " profit rentals that London
theatres produce. They point to the (apparently)
extravagant salaries paid to certain actors and
actresses. They point to the huge sums spent
by certain managements in producing foolish
plays, and they say that a business responsible
for such profits and such expenditure ought not
to squeal at a system of taxation that costs
the theatre world nothing, but merely makes a
demand upon the pockets of the public.

What are the facts ? Profit rentals on a considerable scale do exist in the theatre world.
Certain theatrical managements are making
comfortable profits, despite the Entertainment
Tax. Huge sums are being spent on theatrical

productions, and in certain cases are yielding a handsome return. When we admit all this, what has it to do with the question of taxing the entertainments of the public ? The Entertainment Tax affects the managers indirectly ; it affects the public immediately. Why look at the matter so much from the theatrical managers' point of view ? The public has a right to be considered. Playgoers are showing their dislike to the Entertainment Tax by staying away from the theatres, except in a few certain successful instances. The theatrical profession never suffered so much as it is now suffering from unemployment and general depression.

I object to the Entertainment Tax just as I would object to a suggested revival of the old tax upon windows. Too lightly is it agreed that entertainment is a luxury. Entertainment is a necessity. It is the window of existence. When people shut entertainment out of their lives, they cease to experience any joy from sensible recreation, and fail in sympathy with such intellectual (or unintellectual) refreshment as the theatres provide. They have then nothing in front of them but darkness and stupidity — apathy and atrophy. Theatre haters are

usually brainless and unimaginative beings,
with no brightness in their lives and no real
happiness in their souls. Good theatres act as
windows—they let light and sunshine into our
lives.

Admit, if you like, that the theatre is a luxury,
and say that upon that ground it deserves
taxation : why should it be singled out above
other luxuries for a direct and special taxation,
payable in addition to an income tax already
burdensome enough ? I could form a list of
a hundred and one different luxury businesses,
all of which would be productive of revenue,
and each of which has less claim to exemption
from this irritating form of taxation than has
the theatre. But two wrongs would not right
the matter. The Entertainment Tax should
come off.

We are referred by defendants of this tax to
taxation of theatres on the Continent. We are
told that the public in France and Germany,
etc., has to pay a tax for theatre-going, and that,
therefore, what is justifiable in France, Germany,
etc., can with equal equity be applied in England.
What are the conditions on the Continent ?
The theatrical manager abroad is given the

opportunity of keeping his theatre open on
Sundays. Upon that day he gives two performances, both of which are usually crowded to the
doors, and it is upon the proceeds of those Sunday
performances that he relies for paying his Entertainment Tax for the whole week and for carrying on at a profit. If you are going to say to
the English manager that he must not keep his
theatre open on the one day in the week when
he can be certain of filling it, if you cannot see
your way to give the English theatrical manager
an opportunity by additional Sunday revenue of
meeting the increased costs that have assailed
him in every direction, you cannot sustain the
argument that Continental methods are applic-
able here. No Sunday shows, no Entertainment
Tax—should be the theatrical managers' plea to
the Revenue Authorities and the Government.
Allow Sunday shows—you increase the revenue
from the tax, and you can reduce unemployment in the profession by a stipulation that
the workers in the theatre shall have one
day's rest a week.

The running expenses attached to every
theatre have trebled themselves, yet the Entertainment Tax equals on the average 20 per cent.

of the gross takings. As a tax it is grossly unfair to the theatrical manager, not only for the reasons I have given, but also because it has to be collected by the manager himself. He is given the trouble of handling, remitting and filling up forms. He has to make, without being paid for doing so, thousands of clerical entries in respect of each theatre he controls, and even upon weeks when the theatre receipts show a heavy loss and involve him in financial embarrassment he still has to collect and hand over the tax. The artists who are responsible for the entertainment may have to do without their salaries. The tax will still have to be paid. A recent instance of this occurred in London. The Government appropriated the salaries of the players, who are still waiting to be paid by the defaulting manageress !

Of course, there is a lot of undesirable entertainment in the theatres, but how does that affect the question ? The main influence of the theatre is uplifting and moral. I do not know how many thousands of pounds in taxes the Gilbert and Sullivan operas have been responsible for handing over to the Government, but I think it little short of scandalous that such a clean, wholesome, stimulating, and joyous means of brightening one's outlook should be selected for a system of special taxation merely on the ground that it is " amusement." The success of the operas in spite of the tax is no evidence in the tax's favour. The idiot who first conceived the Entertainment Tax ought to be put upon the list of Gilbert's " Mikado." He never would be missed.

VII

ON AUDIENCES

OUR best beloved actress, Ellen Terry, has been discussing the reform of the Theatre. In her view audiences are in far greater need of reformation than the theatre itself. If the public gets the kind of play it wants, there may be something in her contention. But does it? Mr Anthony A. Ellis has been explaining the difficulties the commercial manager of good intentions has to meet, and echoing Miss Terry in blaming the " big, intelligent, careless, capricious public which accepts all too readily the standards set for it."

The public is broad-shouldered and can afford to listen to such complaints with indifference, and Mr Ellis and all his brethren may equally disregard Mr William Archer's indictment of their enterprises as " gambling hells." The fact remains that you can no more reform audiences without good plays and brilliant acting than you can inspire congregations without great preachers and fine sermons. Devout listeners may create dull lectures. Acquiescent, uncritical audiences will certainly make for stupid plays.

While on this subject of audiences, let me here explain, as one who has watched a different audience viewing the same play for hundreds of nights in succession, and as one who has tried to make a special study of audiences as of plays and actors, that audiences are never the same for two nights running. They vary in their moods, their ideas, their character, even as do individuals. Ask any comedian whether he can always rely upon getting the same degree of laughter at the same point in the action or on the same sentence in the dialogue. Ask any emotional actress if with exactly the same effort and the same material she can arouse two audiences to precisely the same pitch of enthusiasm. " How are they to-night ? " is the first question the waiting performer at the wings has to ask one who has taken the plunge, very much as one expectant bather enquires from another the temperature of the waves.

It is true that in the old days, when certain theatres were identified with fixed policies, the audiences assumed a certain character in each theatre, but that was largely because the same playgoers went night after night, and each theatre had its own *habitués*. To-day the floating population of the great city floats more irregularly and erratically than ever it did. The tastes of the playgoer are more elusive and more catholic, and very much as second-hand book lovers ramble eagerly over the amazing mixtures provided on the stalls with equal zest, so you will find the patron of the theatre of our times one evening frequenting musical comedy, another evening the poetic drama, and still another watching the modern Society play with the same degree of listless tolerance.

As for reforming audiences, I wouldn't have them altered for the world. They are constantly reforming themselves. Like the Athenians of old, they are ever in search of the new thing. They are never the same in their longings and desires for six months together. They never fail to respond to the human touch. Sometimes they are blind to wit and humour ; at other times they wish for nothing else. Sometimes they like their meat highly seasoned; there are periods when it must be cold and served with salad in a state of nature. Like the dear creatures who fill the better part of our lives, they are only constant in their wish for change. The high priestess of the theatrical temple may sigh for an alteration in the hearts of the people. Her sighs are vain. The hearts of the people are the same as they were when she was young and had the world before her. Only the Oracle is silent for the moment.

VIII

"THE PLAYBOY OF THE WESTERN WORLD"

IF an Englishman had written this play he would have been shot within twenty-four hours of its production. And he would have deserved it. But because it comes from an Irish poet, because it is so genuinely Irish in its perversity, its sense of ridicule, its charged realism, its squalor, its shebeenery, and its curious streaks of romanticism, its black-hearted treachery to Irish ideals, it is hailed as Heaven-sent genius. The case of Ireland at this moment is being judged by the world. She stands at the tribunal of the nations and waits for her fate to be decided. And this is the moment selected by Irishmen to revive "The Playboy of the Western World." Well, well!

The Irish who howled this play down and who went into mad furies when it was first played in Dublin, Liverpool, Philadelphia, New York, and elsewhere were not such fools and vandals as they have been made out to be. To reproach them for having had no sense of humour is ridiculous. A play that cannot be performed without shocking the pride and sensibilities of Irish people, whatever part of the world they find themselves in, must have some devilish and damnable quality in its composition akin to sin itself. "The Playboy" was the product of a great brain soured by illness, made morbid by disease. It is the kind of enigmatic rollick indulged in by a doomed consumptive—the feverish and forced joviality of a man faced with his own coffin.

The stupid, short-sighted folk who wonder why so many Irishmen have revolted at it cannot see that there has been no more shameful betrayal of the Irish character at its worst than this terrible indictment of it by one of their own countrymen. He deliberately selected the worst traits of the worst kind of Irish peasantry. Synge pictured the people in a village on a wild coast in County Mayo, and he pictured them as ignorant, crime-worshipping, drunken, bestial peasants who all, without one solitary exception, are eager—fanatically eager—to exalt the parri-

cide—or the man they think is a parricide—as
a Heaven-sent hero, to exult in the tortures
practised by dog-hangers, ewe-maimers, and
cattle-lynchers. The whole village glories in
murder for murder's sake. Why, in the names of
all the saints, was there not a priest on the
scene, to restore the balance a little ?

This play may or may not be a comparatively
true assailment of the savagery, the barbarism,
the credulity rampant in an Irish village, and
it may or may not be an arraignment consequently of England and England's responsibility
for Ireland ; but I cannot believe in the sincerity
or truth of such a one-sided, narrow view of any
form of humanity. God never made such beings.
They would be disowned by a Frankenstein.
Murder to them—and all of them, remember—
is glorious and wonderful, not because circumstances have made it justifiable, but because
it is in itself and of itself a daring, miraculous,
thrilling, and prancing act.

The native cruelty and brutality of the women
in this comedy make me reel with horror and
aversion. Interest in crime and the criminal is
not confined to Mayo. It has its followers by
the million in this country, in Wales, and even in

Scotland. A portion of the Press can still flourish on the cess-pits, and sends its emissaries broadcast to gather filth on the highways; but would any Englishman be justified in representing an entire English village as soaking themselves in obscenity and indulging in the wholesale idolatry of immorality? I think not. In spite of the *nil nisi* edict, I cannot forbear saying that any Irishman who could paint such a lopsided portrait of a section of his race was not only a liar, but a traitor.

Whatever his motives, the result is terrible. This squint-eyed sarcasm, this myopic sneering is not " vision." And all the glamour of Irish idiom, the quaintness of rhythmic swell in the language, the tonal charm of the brogue will not dispel the acridity, the venom, the falsity of the creation. They call it a joke. Is it a joke to be abnormal, to be spiritually hunch-backed, morally deformed, and mentally deficient? They call it a work of art. There are works of art in Brussels, in the Wiertz Museum. They call it a classic. I admit I do not know a " classic " when I see one. Who does? For it is not our own individual acceptance of a thing that makes it a classic, but the acceptance of the ages, the considered opinion of generations following each other all holding the same view. On the other hand, it is slavish adherence to other people's standards and a fright at your own eyesight and your own reason that convert us into believing in all these so-called "classics."

This piece is as classic as the spud. It smells of the black, rotting earth. The peat still clings to it. It suggests a pigsty—innumerable pigsties—in the vicinity. And the accursed blight of stupidity — the blemishes of passion, laziness, superstition, intolerance, and intemperance, mildew it throughout. It is the whole sum of Irish follies and prejudices concentrated into two and a half hours of entrancing dialogue. It is Irish imagination at its finest pitch prostituted to destroy by mordant and biting humour the faith of a people in themselves. We have been told there are sermons in stones. Synge has cloaked dirt with beauty, covered ignorance with romance, and poetised over crime. For that he may be compared with Shakespeare. But, thank God! we have had no Englishman who has selected all the worst in us and avoided the best in us to show us as he thinks we are.

IX

" ARDEN OF FEVERSHAM "

SOME twenty plays, roughly speaking, have been attributed to Shakespeare, the true origin of which is more than doubtful. Of these, only two—" The Two Noble Kinsmen " and " Arden of Feversham "—can be compared (by reason of their entire composition and their artistic completeness) with the admittedly genuine and acknowledged Shakespearean dramas. The apocryphal always has a spurious, degraded form of interest for us equivalent to that aroused by an accusation of bastardy. There is a false romanticism, a piquing of curiosity in any uncertainty of parentage. Human beings interested in family resemblances and relationary characteristics love to trace similarities of form, manner, or spirit, and these resemblances, real or imaginary, provoke a morbid and unhealthy interest and suspicion such as gossips love and scandalmongers adore.

The apocryphal play is in just the same position as the doubtful heir. Its presumptions can only be founded upon conjecture. Its case can never be proved. However firm the suspicion of its authorship, it bases its claim for recognition upon a suspicion, and must, therefore, be acquitted or condemned in the same mood. "Arden of Feversham" is one of the few apocryphal plays of Shakespeare, the authenticity of which has vexed some of the best minds in Shakespearean study.

Swinburne wrote about it : "Either this play is the young Shakespeare's first tragic masterpiece or there was a writer unknown to us then alive and at work for the stage who excelled him as a tragic dramatist," and in the same essay Swinburne came to the conclusion, after a carefully considered summing up of the arguments for and against, that it was possible for no man's youthful hand to have written it but that of Shakespeare's. With less decisiveness, but with equal readiness of acceptance, commentators like Charles Knight, Delius, and the Dutch translator Quitert, expressed the view that it was an early work of Shakespeare, and in all the clouds of incredulity and distrust raised by Professors Ulrici, Saintsbury, Symonds, Tyrell, Bullen, Bayne, Warnke, Proescholdt, and the rest of the critical authorities who have probed deeply into this fascinating literary question, there is a respect, in fact, an admiration, for the work akin almost to a recognition of its legitimacy.

It is perhaps a platitude to say that the more of actual life a dramatist puts into his plays the more vital they become. " Arden of Feversham " is a play founded upon facts. It was based upon an actual murder, and is, therefore, a dramatic record of contemporary crime. Like the Grand Guignol of the present day, it concerns itself with actual physical horror, and while it does not rise to the level of the highest art, it possesses qualities that mark it unmistakably as the work of a poet, a psychologist, and a dramatist. We must remember that in the days when it was written the newspaper had not come into existence. The theatre was used to a considerable extent as a substitute for the newspaper.

Had the terrible murder of Mr Arden of Feversham been committed last week instead of on February 15, 1550, all the material with

which this quaint old play is loaded, the graphic
and detailed business of the conspiracy and
actual crime, would have found its way at
length into our popular prints, and caused as
great a sensation through a typographical
medium as it did when it was first enacted on
a theatre stage. How intense that interest was
may be judged by the fact that the play was
written forty years after the murder was committed. Were our newspapers to day so belated
in their intelligence they would run considerable
risks of not being bought.

Of course, one has to remember that interest
in the tale had been kept alive by Holinshed's
Chronicle, Stow's *Chronicle*, while the actual
facts are recorded in the "Wardmote Book
of Faversham." The Shakespearean authorship
of the piece was first suggested by Edward
Jacob, a citizen of Faversham, in the year 1770.
It was entered on the Stationers' Register on
April 3, 1592, as "*The Lamentable and True
Tragedie of M. Arden of Faversham in Kent.
Who was most wickedlye murdered, by the meanes
of his disloyall and wanton wyfe, who for the loue
she bare to one Mosbie, hyred two desperat ruffins
Blackwill and Shakbag, to kill him. Wherin is*

shewed the great mallice and discimulation of a wicked woman, the unsatiable desire of filthie lust and the shameful end of all murderers. Imprinted at London for Edward White, dwelling at the Lyttle North dore of Paules Church at the signe of the Gun.   1592."

The story is one of passionate crime. It is a tale of lust, jealousy, brutality and murder. Arden has a beautiful but disloyal wife. Through love of a certain base-born steward named Mosbie, the wife, by arrangement with her paramour, hires two desperate ruffians, Black Will and Shakbag, to kill her husband, against whom two other men also harbour criminal intentions, and the efforts of all this gang of would-be murderers are, after a series of thwarted attempts, eventually successful. The actual murder is worked out with circumstantial detail, and the construction of the scene shows a knowledge of stagecraft of the highest order. All the characters in the tragedy are clearly and decisively depicted. The Arden is unmistakably a proud gentleman, a man of courage, much nobility of mind, a combination of trustfulness and suspicion, affection, and simplicity. Alice his wife is an extraordinarily interesting and complex study, a dissimulating, lustful, uncertain, temperamental creature, driven to murder by the frantic nature of her guilty desires, but just as firmly and rapidly turned to repentance by aversion to the deed when it is done.

Black Will is an overbearing, gorgeous, richly human figure, drawn with many loving, intimate touches, an unconsciously comic vagabond of the determined criminal type. Shakbag, his fellow scoundrel, is almost as divertingly painted, and just as real. These two scoundrels are professional blackguards, despatchers of men, without a spark of conscience or sentiment. Murder is their trade, to be carried out with all despatch and without nonsense. They have no more scruples for their victim than the butcher has for the ox in the slaughter-house. The only tenderness they possess is for their own safety. But of all this rascally crew, the most despicable is Mosbie, the lover. He never seems to be genuinely in love with Arden's wife. He is always ready to use her for his own selfish advancement, for his ugly passions, and as a butt for his resentment.

She cannot even express sympathy for his wounded arm without receiving a reproach from him that it was she who was the cause of it. Again and again she revolts, but invariably succumbs to his spell. She seems helpless under his will. He always taunts her with any failure of their plans, and by his lying, his servility, his treachery, his impudence and his utter lack of manhood, cuts as pitiful a caper as the worst of Elizabethan lovers.

Arden's friend and counsellor, Francklin, is the most conventionally drawn, whilst the least conventional personage of the drama comes before us in the person of Arden's servant Michael. This lad provides an example of cowardice in excelsis. His is a cowardice that inspires fear in the beholder, a cowardice that ennobles itself by assuming the rôle of Conscience knocking at the door. From a miserable, trembling and shrinking cur evolves a picturesque figure of guilt paving the way for justice by tremulous admissions of its weakness and doubt.

I cannot quite bring myself to believe in " Arden of Feversham " as a tragedy wholly the genuine product of Shakespeare, whether

in his youth, his prime, or his old age. It is
too naked, too unadorned, too savage to be the
complete creation of that master mind. The
direct unexcused and inexcusable criminality
of all the murderers, the coarse and prolonged
indelicacy of the woman's passion for an under-
ling, the comparative absence of subtlety, and
the true psychological insight into human
motives with all their varying details are defects
that for me brand it as unmistakably foreign to
Shakespeare.

As Dr Brandes has pointed out so pertinently,
Shakespeare was fond of representing human
nature as many-sided, with inward develop-
ments and inconsistencies. He did not, after
the Greek and Latin fashion, fix character in
typical form with one dominant trait thrown
into high relief. I can find in " Arden of
Feversham " little of that lyrical charm, that
bird-like readiness to soar into the Empyrean,
that so distinguished even the meanest of his
acknowledged works.

The author of this tragedy is more concerned
with the action and the plot of his tale than
with its embellishments and adornments. He
sings, and the singing makes us stop and listen,

but there is a shame-faced, sneakish, halting feeling that makes us aware of the fact that the dramatist has a job to do and is determined to get on with it. Here and there the music asserts itself, and there are passages where the lilt of the true Shakespearean muse seems to strike the ear with welcome familiarity. This is especially noticeable in parts of the speeches of Alice and Michael. For instance : " So list the sailor to the mermaid's song. So looks the traveller to the basilisk."

If I were asked to believe that Shakespeare retouched this script and put it in shape for the stage I might not feel inclined to dispute the contention.

We must remember, too, that the name of Arden must have had a great fascination for Shakespeare. His mother was an Arden. The Ardens were an old and honourable family which traced its descent back to the days of Edward the Confessor. The forest of Arden has been immortalised by Shakespeare. We do not care whether it was in Warwickshire or in France ; we only know it was the forest of Shakespeare. And listen to Black Will talking to Bradshaw :—

Will. Why, Bradshawe, was not thou and I Fellow-souldiers at Bulloine, wher I was a corporall and thou but a base mercenarye groome? No fellowes now! because you are a gouldsmith and haue a lytle plate in your shoppe! You were gladde to call me "fellow Will," and with a cursy to the earth, "One snatch, good corporall," when I stole the halfe Oxe from John the vitler, and domineer'd with it amongst good fellowes in one night.

Does not such a speech awaken echoes of Falstaffian scenes? For me it does.

The piece acts well, and as representing the earliest form of melodrama, now so popular amongst us once again, its educational value is considerable.

The effect of the play on the whole is one of primitive joyousness, childish zest in the cruelties of life. It has a natural ingenuousness prompting to the smile suppressed.

X

REVUE

IF you were asked to define Revue, could you do so? If you were asked what form of theatrical entertainment was singularly and distinctively associated with our own times, what would you answer? From which two conundrums let me proceed to a third. Why is Revue what it is?

We live in an impatient age. We do not care to, we cannot concentrate for a long while upon one subject. The majority of us at least have no mind to do so. Revue is a concession to the impatient, a recognition of the present call for constant change. It is as much a part of modern life as the cinema, the motor-car, the aeroplane, or wireless telegraphy. There is the same celerity, variety and efficiency in all these things.

In a revue there are no unities. What Aristotle would have said about it I cannot

imagine. We can, through its glasses, survey
mankind from China to Peru in half an hour,
or put a girdle round the earth in forty minutes.
All the moods, all the passions, all the humours
may be ours in an hour.

According to Mr Wimperis, the Highbrow, at
the very mention of revue, " groans and elevates
his nose three semi-tones." But I doubt if Mr
Wimperis is right. My own theory is that
Revue lives upon the Highbrow, who nourishes
a secret passion for it which he furtively and
feverishly exercises at every opportunity. It
allows him to unbend. He can throw off his
pose. You will find more middle-aged, elderly,
philosopher-like gentlemen in the stalls of a
revue than you will find in the Athenæum
members' list. One of the most notable critics,
a man of erudition, refinement and taste, has
confessed a partiality for it that amounts almost
to weakness.

Revue, most modern and specialised of
theatrical conceptions, tries to appeal to all.
Its universality is at the same time attractive
and debasing. It is as a whole almost the lowest
form of stage art ever known, yet it may contain
in its parts the highest efforts of the best artists.

There seems to be a frenzied desire on the part of the revue producer to crowd as many items in of an evening as the time at his disposal permits. He " blacks out " each turn with rapidity; he has no waits between the turns, or if he must have, he invents a comic interlude to beguile the spare moment when the scene is being changed. There are many kinds of " shows " that call themselves revue. There is the series of splendid spectacles costing thousands of pounds to put on. Frequently these are dreams of enchantment, visions of beauty. Frequently they are barren, empty, worthless displays. There is the simply staged, economically dressed revue costing hardly anything but the artists' salaries. This is often the most diverting, and there is the revue where a compromise is sought between the two methods. There is the revue that depends upon the producer, the one that depends upon a solitary artist, and the revue that depends upon the wit of the author.

The ideal revue has yet to be written. Most so-called revues are not revues at all. They are hotch potches—olla podridas—jumbles—variety shows—a series of music-hall turns strung idly and incoherently together or boldly thrown on one after the other without the least attempt at continuity of purpose or consecutive thought. The ideal revue should reflect the temper at the moment, the events of the day, the passing mood of the crowd. It should satirise the follies of the hour, put into the public pillory all the braggarts, publicity seekers, cranks, and pests of society. It should flash the light whip of ridicule and fun around the shoulders of all folks who rush into the limelight and try to monopolise it. And whilst doing its little castigatory jobs it must not forget to be witty, entertaining, and pleasantly alive. There must be jolly music in the air, and nimble, graceful toe work to watch, pretty girls to see wearing rare costumes, and fashion may show her latest pranks, the scenic artist revel in stage fancies. A little drama, a tabloid farce or two, a tragedietta even, and there you have in this extraordinary salad bowl of a thousand and one ingredients the Revue of Revues.

XI

THE FOURTH WALL

I LOVE belabouring an opponent with his own pet club. So, evidently, does Mr Bourchier. It is a practice popular amongst men since the days when we all lived in caves. Mr Bourchier is a clever man. He must know quite well that the Fourth Wall is my " King Charles' Head." I am always dragging it in. He knows, too, that when I objected to the obvious absurdity of two members of his company, supposed to be indulging in a little quiet heart-to-heart talk with each other, seating themselves with full faces turned towards the audience speaking every sentence, not to each other, but to the folks in front, I was attacking a grave abuse of the stage and trying to uphold that very principle of the fourth wall for which he now appears an advocate. I maintain that in his production of " Tiger ! Tiger ! " Mr Bourchier took no heed of any imaginary fourth wall. He allowed his leading

lady to fling her emotions headlong to the
audience in full noticeable consciousness of their
presence, and to my mind the result was—well—
theatrical.

But I forgive him because he has given me
an opportunity of returning to my favourite
topic. Actors and producers are not really to
blame. The proscenium and the present system
of staging are absolute bars to realism and
illusion in the theatre. We must remember
that this picture frame in which we now try to
work was, as an idea, not known more than
three centuries ago. Its only merit is that it
enables authors to cut off instantly the proceed-
ings of their characters by means of a curtain,
and to disclose suddenly a particular scene or
act which they have conceived. Its disad-
vantages are too many to be here detailed. It
induces a tendency to arrange everything in
pictorial form. The producer has to study the
grouping of his people in relation not to nature
but to the superficial area of the proscenium
and the frontal aspect of the aperture it creates.
It compels him to consider scenic effects from
the flat view of an artist or painter ; it limits his
vision and his power of handling situations to

one point of the compass. This cannot be sound artistically or desirable æsthetically, and it must exercise a stultifying and handicapping influence upon his work as a whole. The theatre should reveal the human form from all angles—not only one. The Greeks and Elizabethans were wiser than we in this.

There are certain plays that demand open and obvious contact with the audience. In farce, for instance, it is inevitable and desirable that a certain impudent familiar communication between actor and audience be carried on. With serious plays and pieces pretending to any degree of realism, the only way to treat the fourth-wall notion is to regard the audience in the light of benevolent eavesdroppers peeping through some cranny, crevice, or hole unobserved, undetected by the characters on the stage. The actors must not in the slightest way betray their consciousness of the presence of onlookers. They must know the audience is there, but conceal that knowledge. The spectators must be in the position of gods who watch the struggles and antics of poor humanity without ever indicating the fact that its secret griefs and anxieties are being witnessed. Now, to peep through a keyhole and see a number of people behaving in a room as if they were conscious of your presence on the other side of the door is to put yourself in the position of a discovered burglar or peeping Tom. You at once become ignominious, and so do they. The moment an audience become conscious of the fact that the players are openly appealing to them for their sympathies and interest you may be sure that bad art is asserting itself and theatricality is in the ascendancy.

This is, at any rate, my theory of the theatre. It has to be modified, of course, according to the class of play and the nature of the entertainment. It would be wrong for me to dogmatise and lay down sweeping rules to cover every form of acting. The really great actor, like the great poet, the great musician, or the great artist is subject to no rules except those his own genius imposes. He can successfully over-ride if necessary even the belauded principle of the fourth wall. I am not dealing, however, with the efforts of genius, but with ordinary dramatic craftsmanship. It is from that standpoint that my complaint against the practice of openly and obviously addressing the audience is addressed.

I have so much to say on this subject that I must hope to make it the basis of a future article and to deal at the same time with a number of points raised by my various correspondents, who seem to be vastly interested.

The only defence of the practice in the argument which carries any weight with me is that it enables the actor or actress who indulges in it to make themselves clearly and distinctly heard in every part of the house. Distinct enunciation is a great quality, but if the players know their business they can make themselves heard perfectly and easily even when they turn their backs on the audience, as they have every right to do when the situation demands it.

XII

ON SPEAKING UP

" THERE is a poor man in the back of the gallery who has paid his shilling and wants to hear you." This injunction from the father of a famous actress to his daughter, when she was learning her business, should be painted in golden letters three feet deep in the green room of every theatre. Those terrible interruptions—" Speak up ! " and " Louder, please ! "—have made themselves heard again in our midst, even in our leading theatres. No wonder " boo's " and hisses are finishing some pieces just now.

There is no need to shout. Clear, distinct enunciation and the determination to make oneself heard even in low tones will always assist audibility. The acoustics of many theatres I know are bad. The family circle and gallery are too often constructed without any regard to the fact that the people in them are meant to see and hear. The seats are often uncomfortable, and in some cases cannot be booked in advance. There is all the more reason, therefore, for the player to make his or her voice heard all over the house. The sense of a sentence is, of course, its first importance. Fixing one's mind on the meaning of every sentence means true interpretation. Voice must not be paramount. The just degree of attention must be paid to sense and sound. But sound must not be sacrificed to sense on the stage any more than sense to sound.

" Fluffiness " or forgetfulness of the lines on first nights is far too noticeable. The fate of the theatre depends upon giving fair play to one's author, manager, and audience on a first night. I put a lot down to payment for rehearsals. Fancy paying people for learning their parts ; or rather—for forgetting them.

XIII

" THE CENCI "

WITH what object was "The Cenci" written?
Did its author intend it as a simple tragedy, as
a high effort in poetic drama of a gloomy and
horrifying nature? Was it Shelley's practical
exposition of his revolutionary sentiments? Did
it not represent his intense opposition to
authority and his conviction that man has no
future beyond the grave, and that for the most
part his life is a barren and empty wilderness
in which all kinds of injustice, oppression,
tyranny, and despair can rage unchecked?

In dedicating his tragedy to Leigh Hunt,
Shelley put it forward as " a sad reality." " I
lay aside," he said, " the presumptuous attitude
of instructor, and am content to paint with such
colours as my own heart furnishes, that which
has been." This is not true. The history of
" The Cenci," as shown by Shelley in his play,
was largely imaginary, based on facts distorted

95

or idealised.   The real Beatrice was as shocking a human animal as her degraded father.   The real Count Cenci perpetrated such diabolical infamies that it would be impossible for any dramatist, had he five times the talent of Shelley, to reproduce them on the stage.

It was, therefore, necessary for Shelley to cover the figures and facts of real history with the glamour of his poetry and the gloss of his imagination.   He converted a beast in human shape into a terrible over-powering symbol of aristocratic and domestic tyranny.   He told a story that exemplifies in its clerical intrigue the depths to which religious imposture and tyranny can descend, and the height to which martyred innocence can reach.   But he holds out no hope to the spectators of his play that the victims of this appalling tyranny received compensation in another world.   He suggests no punishment for evil beyond that inflicted by man.   The one idea that looms out largely from the gloom of this drama is the thought that there is perhaps " *no God, no heaven, no earth in the void world— the wide, great, lampless, deep, unpeopled world.*" The idea is forced upon us that " evil must be finally triumphant in the infinite."   At the back of this drama, in short, there is the same spirit that secured Shelley's expulsion from Oxford.

I direct the reader's attention to the final reflections of Beatrice, where, in reply to the exhortations of Lucretia " *to trust in God's sweet love— the tender promises of Christ,*" Beatrice replies, " *Your words strike chill. How tedious false and cold seem all things. I have met with much injustice in this world. No difference has been made by God or man or any power moulding my wretched lot 'twixt good or evil, as regarded me. I am cut off from the only world I know, from light and life and love in youth's sweet prime.*"

These lines seem to me to convey the secret purpose of the author. The general effect of the play is a prolonged wail with one agonising shriek from the human heart, a cry equal to the one so recently raised—" who can forgive God ? " and this effect runs through every scene in the tragedy. It is a violent protest against the idea of a beneficent, all-seeing power controlling the lives and fortunes of individuals. When Beatrice calls upon death to wind her in her all-embracing arms, to hide her like a fond mother in her bosom, and to rock her in that " *sleep from which none wake,*" when she makes her last farewell to her brother there is not one single thought of a future life. She repeats the word " farewell " three times, emphasising and echoing surely the author's own view that death means farewell and nothing else !

I am told that it is a wonderful piece of poetry. I can only reply that there is not a solitary thought in it that has not been anticipated by some other poet. There is not an incident in it that has not been appropriated from some previous drama. Shelley's debt to Shakespeare in the matter of both the words and actions of this piece would fill a column of a newspaper. He took history and altered it to suit his own atheistical purposes and views. He had not sufficient individuality whilst doing so to be anything else than a pale and dull reflection of mightier poets who preceded him.

I could dilate upon my objections to the tragedy, but I prefer to leave it at what I have written.

Miss Sybil Thorndike, by reason of her performance in this tragedy, was declared, " the greatest tragic actress in England." My opinion of her as a serious player was materially improved by this particular representation, but I think

the part is one not wholly suited to her personality or her appearance, and that the actress has
a very long way to go before she will be able to
justify such adulation as she has received. Her
earlier scenes showed an indecision, a nervous
eccentricity that marred much of the beauty
of her performance. I thought her admirable
in the voicing of her wrongs and in the latter
portions of the tragedy after her father's death.
The scene in the court where Beatrice has to
address the wretched Marzio, who has, under
the rack, revealed the secret of her complicity in
the crime, was firmly, eloquently, and nobly
given. It had a dignity, a restraint, and impressiveness that were irreproachable, and her
final speeches were delivered with extraordinary
purity and tenderness.

The general excellence of the acting did not,
however, relieve my mind of the feeling that
I had participated in a retrograde artistic
function. I yield to no one in my admiration
of Shelley as a poet, but I think " The Cenci "
an unworthy product of his brain. It has only
one scene that touches me in any fibre, and it
is full of falsities, shallow and specious thoughts
that fill the ear and paralyse the mind.

XIV

PERSONALITY AND THE STAGE

EVERYONE interested in acting should try to
secure a copy of the late Mr Louis Calvert's
book, "Some Problems of the Actor." It is the
most illuminating guide to the craft I have ever
seen. There are not many works on the subject
worth a moment's attention. No profession is
so neglected from the standpoint of useful text-
books and instructive treatises. The average
theatrical volume is either a collection of dead
criticism, a *réchauffé* of stale stage anecdotes,
or a gushing biography. These are of no practical
value to students of acting.

Calvert was that rare bird, an actor who could
write intelligently about his work. There is
one problem, however, upon which even he is
silent, and it is a problem which has the
greatest pertinence in the present condition of
our theatre. It is the question of personality
versus representation.

What is acting? According to Nuttall, it is the performance of an assumed or dramatic part. Who can in these times agree with such a definition? No one who visits the theatre. You will see Miss Jones playing Miss Jones; Mr Smith playing Mr Smith; and in every part, in every play, you will find personality fitted into character, instead of the assumption and development of character through personality. So sensible is the stage itself of this phenomenon that it distinguishes certain parts as being those set aside for character actors, and terms them character parts. (The odd thing about a character actor is that he is usually called upon to play a person of no character.) As a rule, the character actor is an exaggerated personality who, like his less marked brother, also plays at being himself instead of differentiating, like a true artist, by many nicely observed touches, the character of one person from another. Surely the old actors understood this vital accomplishment better than we do!

Is acting a lost art? Our most successful modern actors and actresses have achieved their positions mainly by exploiting their own individualities, revelling in temperaments, tempera-

tures, and such-like luxuries, and exhibiting
every aspect of their own mental and physical
peculiarities. All very interesting and remarkable, but is it acting ? I can hardly recall one
instance of a great success on the modern stage
where the personality of the performer was
completely hidden, subdued, and merged into
the personality of the part. Granted that this
is a most difficult thing to do, is it not the highest
achievement of the actor ? And should it not
be the principal objective of all who aspire to be
considered actors ? It may be argued that such
acting is only mimicry. That it is not art, but
imitation. That it lacks the true creative
instinct. That the public wish to see their
favourites, and have no interest in portraiture.
Let us see how far such contentions can be
justified.

Ideal acting is surely that which is a satisfying,
idealised reproduction of life. It must not be
confined to a reproduction of another person's
superficial eccentricities and idiosyncrasies. It
must be the complete assumption of another
person's individuality, his actions, feelings,
emotions, sensations. In other words, it should
be a complete projection of oneself into the soul

and body of someone else with the object of exactly portraying that someone else. Such acting seems to me an accomplishment on a much higher plane than the subordination of a part to one's own personality.

This perfection in genuine acting can obviously be attained only after years of hard work and systematic intelligent training. It is a comparatively easy task to drift on to the stage, allow yourself to be fitted with a part by a skilled dramatic tailor, drilled by the stage-manager into a performance nicely calculated beforehand to suit you. It is no distinction for an actor to be selected mainly on account of his appearance and physical suitability because he is " the right type."

I admit that the first essential thing in an actor or actress is to be interesting. I admit that no amount of plasticity will help the performer who is handicapped by an unattractive or unsympathetic stage personality. The chief difficulty confronting the actor of to-day is the theatrical love of routine, the fatal inclination for precedent. An artist makes a big success in a certain type of part. From that day onwards he is doomed for the rest of his life to repeat the same sort of character under a hundred different names. Who is to blame for this? It may be the manager or the actor or the author or the public itself. I do not know.

There is no profession over which so much time and money are spent to so little purpose. There is no other profession which allows the majority of its recruits to grow up anyhow, entirely dependent upon accident, their own circumstances, and without proper guiding hand or adequate direction. It is criminal to waste the splendid talent that we have available in our young actors and actresses in the way that we are doing. Thousands of them go on, year in and year out, spending their days on golf-greens and tennis-courts and their nights in the same insignificant walking on or twenty-line parts, making no effort to improve themselves in their craft, and without seeking or being given the least help from those who are competent to instruct and assist them. To be ambitious as a young man on the stage is, as a rule, to be considered ridiculous. Our provincial stages are too frequently hotbeds of stereotyped and brainless imitations of metropolitan notabilities. If actors make a fortunate hit they at once are

blocked up in the *cul-de-sac* of success. The long
run enriches the pocket, but starves the brain.
We need more repertory companies, more
summer stock seasons.

We have recently seen evidence of a certain
liveliness amongst actors in the formation of
a strong Actors' Association. One of the first
serious objects of this association should be
the improvement of the status of the actor
by making him qualify for his profession.
The Actors' Theatre should be their training
ground. Our greatest actors were not born
great. They had to be made so. And the
earlier you catch your actor for training
purposes the better for him and the public.
Municipal money might be worse spent than
in running stock theatres.

Without in the least disparaging those many
remarkable players whose personalities have
helped them to interesting theatrical triumphs in
bygone days, and whose attractiveness in that
respect will assuredly assist them to many other
personal successes in the future, I venture to
make a humble appeal for a more serious study
of the true inwardness of the actor's part. These
players with marked personalities interest me

enormously, quite as much as they do the general play-going public; but I am an enthusiast for the real actor, the man who can be something other than himself, who can show you that there are no boundaries to the imagination. I do not praise superficial versatility. The best actor is he who can not only strip his own soul bare for your edification, but can give you an insight into the varying and contrasting impulses, thoughts, feelings, and passions that animate other imaginary personages, whom he makes real. I have no use for the star whose Othello is much the same as his Hamlet, whose Hamlet differs very little from his Romeo, and whose Romeo is but a shade removed from his Shylock.

Relentless, unflinching portraiture, complete absorption of character—that should be every actor's ideal. How many of our young actors are contenting themselves with gazing Adonis-like at their own reflections? How many are going out into the world studying human nature and affairs? How many make a point of observing the various types of people, giving their closest possible attention to the art of reproducing living types, and passing on to the public the effects of nature, faithfully conned and noted ? Idealisation is desirable, but that idealisation should always be subjective. It must constantly be borne in mind that art has its foundations in nature, and cannot exist of itself.

XV

MAKING LOVE ON THE STAGE

MAN or woman can only suffer from true love once in a lifetime. When it comes it is all-absorbing—all-consuming. It is subject to no alteration. No passion lends itself so easily, so successfully to the purposes of the theatre. No passion is more easily travestied and rendered ridiculous by actors.

How many players have we to-day capable of showing the grand passion? How many actresses in the Green Room Book of next year show genuine power and conviction in a love scene? I will mention no names. We have seen recently upon our stage an example of what was called a " Great Lover," but the love on that occasion had reached a degenerate and enfeebled period. Cupid had assumed crutches. He was in his old age. One pictured him taking an occasional aphrodisiac to maintain his dying rages. That was not the actor's fault. The

part was so written. A book might be written
upon the erotic influence of stage plays. Ten
others would not comprise all that could be said
by a new Ovid on the art of making love as
practised in the theatre.

For love is one of the greatest assets of
the drama, be the drama frankly commercial
or shyly artistic. The theatre adores being converted into an Acmonian wood. It is seldom,
of course, that a Manfred or a Cenci in tragic
horror debases the noble passion by perversity,
but Tristan and Isolde, Paolo and Francesca,
Lancelot and Guinevere—no worshippers of
Chemos these—and scores of others troop in a
beautiful and bewildering procession in lingering
pageantry exquisitely into the memory. Love,
be it sacred or profane, has a perpetual hold
upon our attention. It is our cause, our origin.
There was a time, perhaps, when we ourselves
played Romeo. At a later stage, perhaps, came
Antony. Life has, perhaps, at one moment put
us in the position of a Joseph. We may have
once felt the thrill of love at first sight. The
little Western flower has been worn in our button-
hole. Or Kama, the rose of the East, may have
kissed us in our sleep.

But where shall we look to-day for the tender, the soft, the gentle truth of the love of a Sweet Lavender or a Little Minister ? The modern stage concerns itself greatly with love in its meanest and ugliest aspects. We had an example of that in "The Circle." Our youngsters are taught to make love unwillingly, shamefacedly—with no tremendous abandonment such as great love demands. We have just seen in London how Frenchmen make love upon the stage. They put it on and off as they do their gloves. But they do it so gracefully and with such an air that we can watch them for ever without wearying. They do not in their frenzies make us think of garlic or goose-grease.

Some of our older comedians—those who have just passed the middle age—can still make love irresistibly. There are at least five mercurial gentlemen—they need no free advertisement from me—whose Camdeon twilight still outshines the morning glare of all our younger lovers. They do not suffer from effeminacy, from affectation. Their attack is full of vigour, dash, *élan*. In the rush of their devotion they preserve control. They master the humour of love and ride triumphantly home with their victim slung to the saddle.

To convey real love upon the stage is so difficult. Its delicate intimacies, its husk of privacy, are so hard to communicate without a shattering—a breakage of the spell. How much easier can hate be shown ! Aversion needs little help from an author. Repulsion can be shown by a single gesture—a solitary grimace. Love is so near the border-line to insanity. That is why it is such fine groundwork for farce. Love-making can be most farcical when it intends to be most serious.

I watched a piece of stage-courtship one evening last week. The actor looked hungry— devoured up with desire. He had a bleary, sodden look as of one doped or drunk. His love took the form of vacant obsession—the fullness of emptiness. He pawed his lady-love unpleasantly. He was sensuous to the limit. He dropped his voice so low in his passion that it seemed as though he had lost it. He had the transports of a wild animal only restrained by a stiff shirt and high collar. He overworked his eyelids. To be especially ineffable with half-closed eyes—he practised butterfly kissing continuously. His lips were for ever pursed like a man about to suck squash through a straw.

He provoked misogyny by his absurdity. Yet no doubt our flappers find him a marvellous stout fellow. His photographs sell by the score.

It is such acting as his, however, that must have provoked Mme. Yvette Guilbert to declare that ordinary men in an audience shrank tiredly away from witnessing a parody upon the act of love. It needs no subtlety of feeling to bring about contempt or amusement at such antics. English actors think it wiser to suggest love rather than give full expression to its emotions. They go to the lengths, some of them, of being openly rude, callous, and hostile to the presumed object of their affections. This form of love-making is easy and simple. It need not reach the " kicking downstairs " stage. It is a dissemblement, and as such, eminently theatrical, modern, and paradoxical.

Your great stage lover can demand any fee from us. Bernhardt at her best, Terry at her best, Duse at her worst—what delirious joys in recollection these names awaken in conjunction with the word love ! Love is an open sesame in the theatre as out of it. We must never lose the art of making love—upon the stage.

XVI

MACBETH AND PREDESTINATION

THE basic idea of Macbeth may be clear to some people. It seems a little hazy in nearly all the commentaries prepared after great thought and labour by Shakespearean professors and actors of repute. I have read, I think, nearly all published opinions on the point, and the views expressed both upon the play and the characters of Macbeth and his wife vary widely and strangely. It is, therefore, not surprising that my views should provoke differences. I do not dispute Lady Macbeth's importance in this tragedy. I look upon her as an instrument of the fate that pursued Macbeth before he married her, and which doubtless drove him into her arms. I do not dispute Macbeth's ambition. I have in all my references to the tragedy drawn special attention to it. A man, however, may have an overweening ambition, and yet, for dramatic purposes, be represented by the author as driven by his destiny into tragedy, ambition being only one of the many factors forcing him to his fate.

I have no wish to make myself clear to " the initiated " ; that would be a work of supererogation, but for those who do not pretend to know anything about the matter, let me say just this —I am not a fatalist. I do not believe that Shakespeare was a fatalist. I see very little evidence of fatalism in his plays, but I hold the view that Macbeth is a tragedy of destiny, and I am prepared to support that view not by any historical distortions or crazy theories evolved out of my own imagination, but by references to the text itself as handed down to us. The text may be, and probably is, unreliable, but it is the only thing we ought to work upon. According to the text of the play the Witches foresaw and foretold Macbeth's fate. Anything that can be foreseen and foretold in the way that the Witches foresaw and foretold things must have been pre-ordained.

The circumstantial detail accompanying the prophecies of the Witches in Macbeth is so overwhelming as to make it perfectly clear to the simplest intellect that the Witches had a knowledge of the future.

Before coming to the particular lines in the text upon which I base my opinion, I must also declare that, as a dramatic critic, I have no concern whatever with the historical uncertainties pranking as facts which Shakespeare himself treated with the same scorn and disregard as I do. I judge Shakespeare solely upon his plays as handed down to us. The rubbish that he was accustomed to throw in for their foundations may be dug up and sorted out by dustmen; I have no use for it. Let us come now to the text :—

Act I. Scene 1.

Second Witch. When the battle's lost and won.
Third Witch. That will be ere the set of sun.
First Witch. Where the place ?
Second Witch. Upon the Heath.
Third Witch. There to meet with Macbeth.

(These lines clearly convey that the Witches knew that Macbeth would finish his battle with Macdonald before sunset—that he would emerge with his life and victorious, and that he would be met by the Witches on the blasted heath. The Witches could foresee those things, therefore they were events which had been settled for Macbeth by Fate, and must have been beyond his control.)

Act I. Scene 3.

First Witch. All hail, Macbeth! hail to thee, thane of Glamis.

Second Witch. All hail, Macbeth! hail to thee, thane of Cawdor.

Third Witch. All hail, Macbeth! that shalt be king hereafter.

(These prophecies indicate that the Witches foresaw Macbeth's rise from Thane of Glamis to King of Scotland. As Banquo puts it, they greet Macbeth with " great prediction of noble having and royal hopes." Banquo implores them on his own account if they can " look into the seeds of time " to prophesy to him, Banquo, also.)

Third Witch (to Banquo). Thou shalt get kings, though thou be none.

(This is clearly a pre-vision of the ultimate ascension to the throne of Banquo's descendants. Again Fate's decision seen and revealed by a witch.)

These revelations so stagger Macbeth that he addresses them :—

Say from whence you owe this strange intelligence ? or why upon this blasted heath you stop our way with such prophetic greetings ?

Act I. Scene 5.

Lady Macbeth. All that impedes thee from the golden round, which *fate and metaphysical aid* doth seem to have thee crown'd withal.

(Even Lady Macbeth cannot avoid referring to *Fate.*)

Act II. Scene 3.

Lennox. Strange screams of death ; and prophesying, with accents terrible of dire combustion and confused events new hatch'd to the woful time ; the obscure bird clamour'd the livelong night ; some say, the earth was feverous and did shake.

(More prophecy. But of what ? The happenings of Fate or Lady Macbeth's indigestion causing an attack of somnambulism ?)

Act III. Scene 1.

Banquo. Thou hast it now ; king, Cawdor, Glamis, all, as the weird women promised, and I fear thou play'dst most foully for't.

(Even Banquo thinks that Macbeth worked his wicked way because the weird women suggested the evil course. He hopes they will prove " oracles " in his own case, so that he may be " the root and father of many kings." It is clear that, whether Macbeth played foully or not—if the weird women only spoke the truth,

Banquo would beget a line of Kings and Macbeth would be Glamis, Cawdor, and King.)

Act III. Scene 5.

Hecate. How did you dare to trade and traffic with Macbeth in riddles and affairs of death, and I the mistress of your charms, the close contriver of all harms, was never call'd to bear my part.

(Hecate, the Queen of the Witches, is angry because the three witches have repeated to Macbeth behind her back all that she as " the Contriver of all Harms " had planned for him.)

At the pit of Acheron meet me i' the morning; thither he will come to know *his destiny.*

(If Macbeth's destiny was not decided—how could he learn it ?)

This night I'll spend unto a dismal and a fatal end. Great business must be wrought ere noon.

He shall spurn fate, scorn death, and bear his hopes 'bove wisdom, grace, and fear, and, you all know, security is mortals' chiefest enemy.

(Hecate laughs at Macbeth's scorn of those inevitable things, Death and Fate.)

Act IV. Scene 1.

First Apparition. Macbeth ! Beware the Thane of Fife ! Dismiss me : enough.

(Why beware the Thane of Fife ? Because he was the man destined to kill Macbeth.)

Second Apparition. Laugh to scorn the power of man, for none of woman born shall harm Macbeth.

(Macduff was ripped from his mother's womb. An equivocation by a witch's apparition who could see that Macbeth was fated to be killed by Macduff.)

Macbeth. I'll make assurance doubly sure, and take a bond of Fate.

(Macbeth is not content to rely upon the Witches' prophecy. He will try to kill Macduff, but fails to do so, thereby unconsciously and unknowingly fulfilling the prophecy.)

Third Apparition. Macbeth shall never vanquish'd be until Great Birnam wood to high Dunsinane hill shall come against him.

(A remarkable prophecy of a bit of early Scottish camouflage, impossible to foretell unless the witch's third apparition had the gift of seeing what was preordained.)

Macbeth. Shall Banquo's issue ever reign in this kingdom ?

(Then comes the vision of the eight kings— some of them with twofold balls and treble sceptres, thereby foretelling the union of Scotland with England.)

Act IV. Scene 3.

Malcolm. Macbeth is ripe for shaking, and the powers above put on their instruments.

Act V. Scene 3.

Macbeth. The spirits that know all mortal consequences have pronounced me thus.

Act V. Scene 7.

Macbeth. They have tied me to a stake ; I cannot fly, but bear-like, I must fight the course——

It is idle for anyone to describe the foregoing matters as embroideries. They constitute the pith and essence of the play, and the only possible escape for anyone who holds a contrary opinion is to assert that all the Witches' scenes, and especially the scene where Hecate appears, were written not by Shakespeare, but by Middleton, and that they were only inserted as an afterthought into the tragedy of Macbeth. But how can anyone study the foregoing excerpts as they appear in the play itself and successfully avoid the conclusion that fate, destiny—call it what you will—played the controlling part in Macbeth's career ? The Witches foresaw not only everything that happened to Macbeth, but everything that happened down to the days of James I., for whom Shakespeare wrote the play.

Shakespeare knew that the view of witchcraft expressed in this play would please the King. He knew that these references to second sight would please all the Scotsmen who were then crowding London in connection with the King's accession. Moreover, King James had written a book on Demonology, and was bent upon killing old women all over the place, in the crazy belief that they were witches. Shakespeare wrote his play for the same reason as Mr Bernard Shaw might have written " Heartbreak House," merely because he thought it dealt with a topical subject which would interest the people of his time.

The idea that Lady Macbeth was the sole cause of the trouble is a truly feminine opinion, but is unsupported by the text, see Act I., scene 7—Lady Macbeth : " What beast was't then that made you break this enterprise to me ? When you durst do it, then you were a man ; and, to be more than what you were, you would be so much more the man. Nor time nor place did then adhere, and yet you would make both." What do these words mean ? They must mean that Macbeth first of all suggested to Lady Macbeth the murder of Duncan. He put the evil deed into her mind, and then pretended to run away from it, manlike, leaving her to have the odium of Adam's original plaint—" The woman tempted me and I fell."

It would take far too much time and space to give in these columns extracts from all the eminent authorities upon the fatal and pre-destined aspect of Macbeth, but I hope I shall be allowed to quote the following representative opinions :—

Hazlitt. Macbeth himself appears driven along by the *violence of his fate* like a vessel drifting before a storm. . . . He is not equal to the struggle with Fate. His speeches and soliloquies are dark riddles on human life baffling solution and entangling him in their laby-rinths. The whole play is an unruly chaos of strange and forbidden things where the ground rocks under our feet. Fate and metaphysical aid conspire against his virtue and his loyalty. We can conceive no one to play Macbeth properly, or to look like a man that had encountered the Weird Sisters. The witches of Macbeth are ridiculous on the modern stage, and we doubt if the Furies of Æschylus would be more respected.

Chas. Lamb. From the moment that their (the witches') eyes first meet Macbeth's, he is spellbound. That meeting sways his destiny. He can never break the fascination.

Coleridge. In the grandeur of tragedy, Macbeth has no parallel till we go back to the Prometheus and the Furies of the Attic stage. . . . It would lead me to suspect our great dramatist to have been a studious Greek scholar.

Brandes. Immediately after the murder he is attacked by hallucinations of both sight and hearing and is hounded on, wild, vacillating and frenzied from crime to crime. He defends himself with the hopeless fury of " the bear tied to the stake." The supernatural beings are distinctly conceived as having a real existence outside the sphere of hallucination.

Ulrici. The will of man is not absolutely free self-determination with the full and clear consciousness of its motives. It is rather only conditionally or relatively free, determined by these dark, involuntary and unconscious influences which are the result of the general position of affairs.

Dowden. The weird sisters . . . may take their place beside the terrible old women of Michael Angelo, who spun the destinies of man. Shakespeare is no more afraid than Michael Angelo of being vulgar . . . (they) remain terrible and sublime. They tingle in every fibre with electric energy, their malignity is inexhaustible. There is a terrible correspondence established between the baser instincts of his (Macbeth's) own heart and the certain awful external genius of evil. . . . We are in pain until the horrible necessity is accomplished.

Masefield. He (Macbeth) dies with a courage that is half fury against the Fate that has tricked him.

Bradley. He (Shakespeare) may have seen in the bloody story of Macbeth a subject suitable for treatment in a manner somewhat nearer to that of Seneca or of the English Senecan plays familiar to him in his youth than was the manner of his own mature tragedies. The witches doubtless are romantic, but so is the witchcraft in Seneca's Medea.   Shakespeare must have found a model in Seneca. Parallels between Seneca and Shakespeare seem to be more frequent in Macbeth than in any other of his undoubtedly genuine works. See also Cunliffe on the influence of Seneca on Elizabethan tragedy.

Schlegel. Little more than the mere execution of the crime falls to the share of Macbeth. He is driven into it as it were in a tumult of fascination. He is now fairly entangled in the snares of Hell. We might believe that we witness in this tragedy the overruling destiny of the ancients represented in perfect accordance with their ideas. The whole originates in a systematical influence to which the subsequent events seem mentally linked.

I have only discovered one man who does not in the main support the theory of a Macbeth struggling with Fate. He is Professor Goggin, who argues that the witches are merely mysterious beings who lie in wait for human frailty and urge on mankind to sin and guilt, without the power to control human action or regulate the future. This seems to me such a flat contradiction of the text itself that it calls for very little reply. I have only to refer to Hecate's speech to find a completely different representation of the witches' power.

XVII

UPON CASTING

PLAYS are generally made or marred in the casting. There are, of course, dramatic pieces that are " cast proof." There are comedies that cannot be killed by the actors, and there are farces that act themselves, but in the main the dramatist's success or failure depends chiefly upon the selection of the right players for the portrayal of his parts. The best of theatrical compositions can be made to appear foolish by inept or incorrect rendering, or made uninteresting by inefficient or uninspired interpreters.

Take, for instance, a drama that calls for the spirit of youth. It may be possible to show how juvenile Miss Evangeline Elderblossom remains in spite of her forty-eight summers, it may enchant the aged patrons of the play-house to observe how sprightly and lad-like old Mr Guy Roamer remains notwithstanding his sixty winters, but a pathetic absence of real springtime in their performances will paralyse the author's efforts. He cannot succeed in the face of such an obstacle as Anno Domini.

But neither authors nor producers are always the best judges as to how a play should be cast. Some of the most surprising successes come by chance or by a sudden and unconsidered alteration of plans compulsory or temperamental. No business is so subject to the moods of men and women. No profession is so liable to have all its plans miscarry as is the business or profession of play-producing.

The actor requires a deal of patience. He must wait for his opportunity. The whim of an actress, the caprice of a stage manager, the drunken decision of an outside backer, may place him in control of his future. Never, or hardly ever, will he be in the position of deciding as " captain of his soul " what parts he shall play and what effects he can make with them of his own volition.

And in casting a play not only has the fate of each player to be decided, but the effect actors have on each other must be weighed up. Miss A can never act with Mr B, and Mr C finds the methods of Mr D insupportable. Miss E and

Mrs F are absolutely incompatible, and Mr G refuses to act in any play unless Miss H is given a chance of showing the depths of her utter incompetence. Such is the hopeless personal puzzle that has to be solved by the caster of plays.

I beg of you to remember, Mr Playgoer, that the drama or comedy you are watching may not be in the least like the original conception of the author. The greatest of plays take upon themselves different aspects with each fresh genius who essays to elucidate them for you. The playwright may have dreamt of a hero with characteristics entirely unlike and foreign to those now displayed before you. The real problem of his play may have been blue-pencilled at the dress rehearsal. Mr Blank may have forgotten at the crucial moment the most important lines in the comedy, or he may have spoken, owing to an indulgence in wine or women, or perhaps both, lines belonging to another personage of the piece.

There are producers who go for type, to the exclusion of all capacity for " acting " or " impersonation." " Give me the right type," they will say, " and *I* will do the rest." They make their actors automata and train them to the last gesture.   Other producers allow their players so much rope that they invariably hang not only themselves, but author and producer as well.   But " types " are of no use without the ability to act.   I can understand the attitude of those noted dramatists who refuse to allow certain of their plays to be performed until they can be satisfied as to the cast.   For it is on the cast most plays depend.

XVIII

THE SUNDAY THEATRE

ABOUT this question of opening the theatres on Sundays. I am an advocate of actors' rights. I have been an actor myself, or rather I have gained my living by pretending to be an actor, which is all that the majority of so-called actors can legitimately claim. But I cannot see where the actor is going to suffer. On the contrary, I think the actor stands to gain all.

Mr Bernard Shaw is reported to have asserted that he was occasionally entirely in earnest. No doubt he is earnest in his desire as a social reformer to see the theatres closed on a Sunday, and in his desire as an author drawing fees to see them open on that day, but why should he imagine that the financial gain (if any) will be limited to managers and authors? Theatrical managers are having very rough times just now. Despite their enormously heavy expenses and the slackness of trade, they are carrying on bravely, some of them helping to fill Mr Shaw's pockets with royalties. If they want to keep their theatres open on Sundays in order to meet the competition they are faced with from cinemas and lecturers, why should they not be permitted to do so ? How many actors are there unemployed just now ? How many ex-Service men out of work ? Why not open the theatres on Sundays and employ some of those people who during the week have had no employment ?

Mr Shaw and those who think with him believe that they are studying the workers' interests by keeping theatres closed. Are the public-houses open ? Are the newspapers open ? Are not Atheists allowed to assemble their audiences and revolutionaries permitted to preach on Sundays ? Are not the music halls, the picture galleries, the tea shops, the tobacconists, the concert-rooms open, and the railways, trams, and 'buses working ?

Mr Shaw has a great admiration for the Teuton. Are not theatres open in Germany on Sunday ? Is it not possible to see the French classics acted in Paris on a Sunday ? What Continental capital would make itself ridiculous by such narrow-minded bigotry as we display in this ?

In my view the closed Sunday theatre is typical of that exploded spirit of Puritanism that gave way at the Restoration, with its orgy of vice reacting from a too rigid control of people's behaviour.

It is permitted to be hypocrites in this country. We may have our Sunday theatre so long as we pretend to be a club or society, and pretend also that ours is only a " private " performance. Members of the Actors' Association may act in indecent and improper plays without pay for a crew of long-haired, lantern-jawed, æsthetic freaks, but the moment it is suggested that players should act openly and be paid for their services by Mr Bourchier and his like, howls arise on every hand, even from the Actors' Association itself, which is formed to look after actors' interests.

The financial side of this matter is its smallest. This age has been taught to look upon work as something to avoid. It would shirk work on a weekday if it could. It has lost the honest joy and pride in working for work's sake. It is filled with envy, selfishness and dislike of the other fellow " getting rich."

The public is not being sufficiently consulted

in this question. The business man, instead of having to rush off from his office to the theatre, could look forward with pleasure and leisure really to enjoy a play if the theatres were open. His mind would be free to cònsider it. When wretched weather spoils the Sunday afternoon, as it usually does in this climate, what are most English people driven to ? Sleep after a heavy midday meal.

No one is so well able to work on a Sunday as the actor. For every player in work there are five " resting." Some " rest " continuously, and are only " actors " by courtesy or in the columns of the *Era*.

The average actor in an established West-End success seldom works longer than twenty-four hours a week, whilst the average successful professional man works about sixty hours in the time, and the workman about forty-eight.

As for the working staffs of the theatres—a special Sunday staff could be organised and drafted in by the trades union from the many unemployed hands on their books.

It is also possible to give the whole staff and company of actors a holiday on the Monday or some other ordinary day instead of the Sunday.

XIX

ON CHARM

I SPEAK, of course, of charm in acting. It is an interesting topic. How many capable actresses, how many fine actors, have failed in their careers for lack of that one quality—charm! How many mummers, contemptible otherwise, have built up a reputation and a fortune upon its all-sufficient and all-conquering power! What is charm? It is that sweetness, that amiability of manner, that delicacy of disposition, that refinement of sensitiveness, that personal fascination that, combined into the human mould, make the metal most attractive. The mere capacity to smile has no real place in charm. I have known players who could never smile to be irresistible in their charm—invincible in their witchery. Most of the "charming" players have bad memories. I have often wondered why. Probably because they are so intent upon the present they forget the past.

There are some young men and women whose stage careers I watch with a pathetic interest, just as I might the voyage of some adventurous canoe around a whirlpool. I know that they are doomed. They move well. They speak well. They are conscientious. They have a degree of personality. But they will fail as actors or actresses. Why ? Because they lack charm. And it is so dreadful to think of, because charm is not a quality that can be cultivated. It must be there.

It distresses me to see so much talent almost completely wasted because it has not this peculiar individual temper of charm. I have one actress in my mind whose achievements have been considerable. I have heard her described as a " great " artist. In light or serious work she is equally capable. Her memory is prodigious. Her tragic force considerable. Yet in her this indefinable, elusive, subtle, and persuasive element we label charm is practically absent. Her future is therefore marked with some certainty. She must end in despair.

Men without charm may be sure of a living upon the stage. They cannot expect much more. The charm of a Forbes-Robertson is not for all. It would be deplorable were it so. The young actor who has a charming personality may mumble his words, and betray no intelligence whatsoever, he has yet within his reach heights of public favour to which a Vezin or a Willard could never aspire. I think as I write of a comparatively young man whose name is upon everybody's lips. He was a bad actor when he started. He moved awkwardly. He looked effeminate. He was invariably " soppy." Yet, upon the strength of his charm, he has worked his way rapidly to the front, until now he promises to become that worst of catastrophes theatrically—a popular actor.

I have a grievance against the " charming actor " that I cannot bear to think about. Invariably he succumbs to the fascination of one part. The public adore him. They fasten upon one interpretation. For them he is so full of charm in it that they never permit the critic to see him in any other. One of our finest living actors (I am not going to tell you his name) is so full of charm, that they keep him in the provinces playing to capacity over and over again the same " charming " part in the same " charming " way. It is lamentable. With ladies the syrenic fascination is more endurable. We expect, we demand charm, and consequently we are not so surprised when it appears in response.

Charm is to the actress as a crutch to a lame man. It helps her to progress. Let me bring to your mind (again without nominal reference) one of the most brilliant young actresses. Her playing is often disfigured by stupidity. She has brains, but is too lazy to use them. She knows she has good looks and that she is popular, and her reliance upon those factors is more confident than her dependence upon the author. Where would she be without her " charm " ? I shudder to think. She just sits back and allows her charm to work for her. It is wonderful.

Some players set out deliberately to capture charm. It cannot be done. Their attempts are painful to watch. We see them ogling coyly their audiences, playing a game of finesse with all the artfulness of which they are capable. Their work is like " new chum " gold. It will not stand the test of analysis. The conscious gropers after charm are worse than those amateurs who look for nothing but a showing off of their own disfigurements.

XX

GILBERT AND SULLIVAN OPERA

I BEGIN to be really annoyed with both Gilbert
and Sullivan. They not only promise to deprive
me of my legitimate occupation as a dramatic
critic ; they are making me feel intolerably
aged. True, I can renew my youth in the
fountain, sparkling and perennially clear, of their
genius. True, too, is it that I can find inexhaustible springs of pleasure in the felicities of
their partnership. But I prefer to enjoy them
mutely, dumbly. They were the friends of my
salad days. They stir up enthusiasms that led
me night after night to visit the same piece, to
wait at gallery doors from early morn till dewy
eve, and commit all those playful imbecilities
associated with the name of playgoer. They
knew my first grey hair. Airs from " H.M.S.
Pinafore," " Patience," or " The Mikado "
accompanied my first search for a job—my
subsequent speedy dismissal from it for incom-

petence and insolence, and my brave attempts to find another.

When I dared the ocean for the first time, I did so with recollections of the Rt. Hon. Sir Joseph Porter, K.C.B., First Lord of the Admiralty. When first I came to Penzance, its principal interest for me lay in the fact that it was the home of Frederic and Ruth, and though I looked in vain for pirate kings and modern major-generals of the pattern of General Stanley and found therein no " cheerful facts about the square of the hypotenuse," it will always be welcome in my memory, because of the story and the music fastened to its name by two magicians of the theatre respectively named Gilbert and Sullivan.

And how many others are there who can echo similar sentiments of painful charm or joyful recollection ? The principal of this artistic combination is the combination itself. It is an ideal partnership. I have heard the librettist contemned as a shallow, acidulated, inverted, out-of-date humorist. I have known the composer to be scorned as a trifler, an unworthy tickler of ears, an empty soulless jingler of artificial melodies. But invariably the man who

has no use for Gilbert is devoted to Sullivan.
The enemy of Sullivan is the friend of Gilbert,
and, failing one or other of these attitudes, we
find our Savoyards dividing their affections and
devotions in equal parts.

The particular form of humour known always
as Gilbertian humour, the comic spirit of topsy-
turvydom (a twist of mind no doubt adopted
in sympathy with Lewis Carroll), has left its
impress, it would appear, permanently upon our
musical comedy stage, and, in fact, upon our
everyday life. Gilbert's phrases have passed
into our language, and his expressions have
become a part of English literature. What
more can any English author hope for ? Gilbert
had his failures like every other librettist, and
very bad failures some of them were, but we
measure a man's talent by his achievements,
by the heights he attains to, and not by his
fumblings on the ladder when he is not quite " in
the vein."

To deal with the music of Sullivan is not
within my province. I can but record the fact
that young playgoers to-day find it as pristine
and as satisfactory as I did when I first heard
it, and that is not quite yesterday.

The qualities of the Gilbert and Sullivan operas are not only enduring ones, they are such as appeal peculiarly to English people. The humour is clean. The hilarity never descends to buffoonery. The satire is pungent, occasionally unkind, but it is tempered by the beneficence of real wit and the soft assuagements of genuine melody.

Properly and adequately to appreciate their works one has to grasp what the musical play was like before their advent. It had descended to a deplorable depth of slimy, indecent degradation, to which our present Revue, banal and disjointed as it so often is, has never fallen.

I often feel whilst I am listening to some of Sullivan's music just like a choir boy. I want to join in. It has a dimly religious influence upon me. When Sullivan went to · Leipzig to complete his musical education, after studying under Sterndale Bennett, his first compositions, so it is said, were strikingly unconventional. But he was attracted by the oratorio, and on his return to England, it was only fortuitous that Burnand's farce of " Box and Cox " first led him into the direction of buoyant and humorous melody. Equally fortuitous was his meeting and first partnership with William Schwenk Gilbert, and when, at the Royalty, on Thursday, March 25, 1875, "Trial by Jury," described as "an original dramatic cantata," was first produced, who then present could have dreamt it was to herald such a brilliant, extraordinary, and lasting series of comic operas such as subsequently issued from the source?

In worshipping at the shrine of this amazing pair, however, theatre-goers must not forget what is also owing to the D'Oyly Carte family in connection with the enterprise. It is all very well to have the book and the music, but without the business capacity that has always distinguished this wonderful D'Oyly Carte trio—father, mother and son—it is, I venture to assert, doubtful whether this Savoy sprout would have grown to such vigorous proportions, and whether it would have ever tided over that difficult transition period when plays cease to be "in the fashion," and require sustaining till the time when they become stock favourites.

Percy Fitzgerald in 1894 recorded the fact that revivals of old plays were too often attended by failure. He wrote that "on each occasion great efforts were made to excel in mounting and decoration all previous displays. It would seem, however," he continued, " to be the form and pressure of the time that revivals rarely answer save under special conditions where the work has been thoroughly appreciated; the very familiarity and the enjoyment of its good things work against it." We appear now to have passed that period and reached a time when revivals of these plays are ever welcome, so long as they are staged in accordance with the traditions of the D'Oyly Carte staging.

What Gilbert taught the stage of his day might well be emphasised in our time. He taught clearness of enunciation, the distinct utterance of every word and syllable, the abolition of slovenliness in gesture, movement, and speech. His martinet spirit of discipline made the English comedy chorus what it is to-day— the best in the world. He taught the virtue of sincerity even in union with absurdity. He never allowed his parts to be spoiled by their performers. Sullivan emphasised the principle of accurately fitting the music to the words, but Gilbert taught the then unpractised habit of fitting each word to the music. His verbal ingenuity was phenomenal. And though his plays bristled and still bristle with topical allusions, nearly all of which have gone out of date, the topicality has become part of the everlasting framework of life, and has made itself history through Gilbert's agency.

I could bring many a smile and many a tear to the middle-aged frequenter of Savoy opera by merely mentioning the names of the many famous players who have sung and acted in Gilbert and Sullivan's operas. There are some who have spent their whole lives doing nothing else. Think of that. Gilbert was surely wrong in saying, as he did, that actors are sufficiently glorified whilst they live. An actor who spends his lifetime in the service of amusing humanity through the medium of such a work as " The Gondoliers," is worthy of whatever glorification the public chooses to offer him.

It is especially interesting at this juncture to recall that Sir James M. Barrie once made a desperate attempt to follow in Gilbert's footsteps with a comic opera. It was called " Jane Annie, or the Good Conduct Prize," and produced also at the Savoy, was written in combination with a scribe who has also since achieved fame in another line of literary work, viz. Sir

Arthur Conan Doyle. It was received at the time as " an astonishing, perplexing phenomenon," and received no prize for its merits. That age had not learnt to understand and love its Barrie and its Doyle as we do. But many other clever writers and composers have attempted to emulate the success of the Gilbert and Sullivan products, and have all failed. There is still hope. We may take consolation from the thought that Gay wrote " The Beggar's Opera," oblivious of the fact that Gilbert would write " The Yeomen of the Guard." That " The Beggar's Opera " and " The Yeomen of the Guard " are still as young as when they first appeared, and that the land that gave us Gay and Gilbert may have other Gays and Gilberts for us in the years to come.

Our librettists and composers must not be hypnotised by the success that has been the lot of these particular authors. They must learn the value of individuality, and find their own. They must not be afraid to be themselves. The slavish adherence to the formulas of others has been responsible for more dullness and stupidity in the theatre than any other factor. Gilbert and Sullivan succeeded because they were individual. They were themselves. They imitated no one. They utilised other men's methods, adopted other men's ideas, but transmuted them into something new, rich, and strange, such as came from no other quarter.

XXI

WHAT IS WRONG WITH THE THEATRE?

THERE is, it appears, something wrong with the theatre. There always is. There always has been. There always will be. A thousand and one different remedies are offered for a thousand and one different supposed complaints. One authority soundly denounces the dramatists. Why don't they write good plays? Another lays the blame upon the managers. They are too commercial. They lack vision, courage, intelligence. The third expert strafes the critics—poor, prejudiced, ignorant, blind stiflers of artistic impulses. The fourth damns the actors. Why don't they act, curse them? If they would only let themselves go. The fifth fellow frets furiously—abolish the actors. Let us have marionettes in their places. Masks are the thing. The buzz of conflicting opinions deafens us. Change the shape of the theatre.

More novelties are needed. Do away with the proscenium arch. Lower the prices. Make the seats more comfortable. Do away with the Entertainment Tax. Send Oscar Asche to Australia. Provide Sunday theatres for the masses. Kill George Robey. Scenery must go. Keep the peerage out of the playhouse. Give us more classics. No marriage for actor-managers. No packed first nights. Abolish the Censor. Countless other cries mingle in the din. Still the British drama atrophies. The critic croaks. The manager groans. The actor golfs. More theatres close. Revivals keep the rest alive, that is those that are not sustained by ridiculous Press stunts or silly farce. When will the British drama actually reach the demnition bow-wows ? It has been on the road to them for centuries.

I am led into this jeremiad, this doleful spirit of interrogation, by two people—Miss Gertrude Kingston and Mr Basil Dean. Miss Kingston is a clever and experienced actress, a manageress in her time, of credit and distinction. The lady has found a new source of the drama's misfortunes. To her mind it is the theatre-goers who are at fault. London, according to her, is now plagued with an increase in its perambulatory population. The public is practising a game of ignorance in regard to the theatre, and the theatre itself has no ideals, no standards of art. The present war-scarred generation has not learnt to appreciate the difference between what is real and what is shoddy in acting. The public does not care about acting. It does not know good acting from bad. " How should it," queries Miss Kingston, " if it has never had the opportunity of comparison ? "

This thoroughly deserved trouncing of public ignorance on the subject of acting makes me chuckle with glee. I find it so true. My profession constantly carries me into the theatre, and I am continually seeing audiences behave idiotically and people raving over performances that have driven me desperate. When the theatre has been ringing with applause I have itched for a steel-studded club with which to brain the players who have been applauded.

There are certain actors and actresses whose totally undeserved popularity has converted them into vain, posturing popinjays, absurdly sensitive to criticism and greedy of praise which they have not merited. Their lack of brains, self-satisfaction, incompetence, disregard of artistic training and experience have made them the idols of the public, who look upon them as Heaven-sent geniuses. Having neither physique, mentality, emotional force, being clumsy in utterance, devoid of music, the product of artistic anæmia, they yet contrive to reach positions where they can insist upon their names being five times as large as anybody else's on the bill, and where the prefixed " and " should be converted into Barrie's " but."

And now let me tell you about something that has not happened to me. Some secret philanthropist has just failed in benefiting himself at my expense. In doing so he benefited me at his own. It was an old trick he tried without success. He had a half-crown grey-paper-wrapped copy of " The Madras House," a comedy in four acts by Granville Barker. In my absence from home my would-be benefactor sent the book by a foolish boy, with a demand for seven shillings and sixpence payment on delivery. The boy stated that it had been sent there by Mr Carroll's orders. There was nothing doing. The play was attractively tied up. It looked worth the cash demanded for it, but there was no money in the house, and its guardian prudently insisted upon retaining the book, saying it would be paid for on Mr Carroll's return home. I have the book, and shall be pleased to meet the sender, but neither book nor seven and sixpence will be forthcoming. I have decided to regard myself on the Free List so far as that book is concerned.

This story has a moral. What our unlucky petty swindler tried to do upon me, many theatrical managers, playwrights, and actors are trying upon the public to-day with a similarly disastrous result. They are seeking to foist off articles worth 2s. 6d. for 7s. 6d., consequently there is never any money in the house.

Now most of you probably know the story about the polite servant of the French dentist who inquired of the patient, " Whom, monsieur, shall I have the misery of announcing." Let me deal with Mr Basil Dean and his utterances about the theatre. I do not propose to, meta-

phorically speaking, draw any of his teeth,
but he delivered a lecture at the Victoria and
Albert Museum the other day entitled " The
Actor and His Workshop." This lecture was
of a provocative nature. It was given in
connection with the international theatre exhibition, and Mr Dean attacked that exhibition
as a glorified example of focussing upon the
means to the end in the theatre rather than
upon the end itself. No one can ever accuse
Mr Dean and his partner of not having given
full value in their theatres. They have followed
the injunction, " good measure pressed down
and shaken together and running over shall
men give into your bosom," and their reward
has been proportionate.

In the theatre, of course, value can never be
tested by reckoning up the total expenditure
of cash. You may have a ten-thousand-pound
production which will only run for seven weeks
and three days. The cleverest of dramatists
must occasionally miss the mark. The interesting actor or actress may miss the opportunity.

To Mr Dean's mind the actor of the present
day is superior in intelligence to the actor of ten
or fifteen years ago, but inferior in emotional

vigour. The younger acting has, he thinks, no
spark in it. Our juveniles could never be guilty
of some of the crude and stupid faults committed
by some of the great actors of the past, but most
of them have either never acquired the breadth,
or, if they ever had any, have lost it in
accommodating themselves to the suppressed
and repressed methods of modern playwrights
and producers. The moving, superbly-controlled
acting force, the wealth of emotional outgiving
so exquisitely developed in the mature art of
Miss Haidee Wright, Miss Rosina Filippi, and Miss
Ellen Terry cannot be seen even in embryo in
the work of most young actresses of the new
schools.

Mr Dean is inclined to attribute this weakness
of method, this inexpressive and over-checked
acting, to the influence of the realistic school.
He blames Ibsen, the translated Ibsen, not the
real one, for much of the existing deterioration
in acting. Many of the plays now produced to
his mind suffer in this way. They lack emotional
force. Their authors seem to regard any display
or exhibition of feeling as matter for ridicule ;
any giving way to anguish or outburst of human
suffering as melodramatic and ridiculous. The

actors are afraid to let themselves go, or if they want to unloosen the reins they are forbidden to do so by their managers. They have become self-conscious, stilted, and unnatural, and the training they have undergone in the class of play that has so long been the fashion has helped to make dummies of them instead of human beings.

This tendency to the suppression of natural emotion and passion has lasted for perhaps twenty years, and in Mr Dean's opinion it is now high time that a richer, fuller, more red-blooded and sincere type of acting was encouraged. The present players are too polite. They should be taught to take the gloves off and show the white heat of actual human passion.

Mr Dean could not bring himself to agree in the least with Miss Kingston in her dictum that the theatre-goers of to-day were no judges of acting. To his mind, acting was an elemental, human, emotional power, and became evident to everybody the moment the right note was struck. It was quite impossible to create something, an effect of anger, pity, remorse—without the actor actually experiencing the feelings he was representing. He had no words in which to despise the actor who indulged in trickery. There were certain well-known performers who came on on the first night with nothing but a bag full of tricks at their disposal. He had been charged with paying undue attention to the material questions connected with the theatre. He would not plead guilty. His main concern as a producer was with the acting. If he could improve the quality and make the sincerity of his actors unquestionable his ideal would be attained.

Outside the acting, he thought the most powerful influence in the theatre was light. With the aid of light the dramatic and emotional portions of the play could be tremendously helped. The vital force in light was indisputable. His ideal of scenery was that it should be so complete and so in harmony with the play that the audience should not notice it was there. The art of actor and of the scene deviser should be welded together by the lighting expert. It was impossible to plan two-dimensional scenery, scenery that had only length and breadth, with three-dimensional scenery, scenery that reproduced length, breadth, and depth. With better stages and more room on our stages, better scenic effects could naturally be obtained. Plays had to be suited to their stages. Shakespeare was seen, or rather heard, at his best on the platform stage. He was an upholder of Bernard Shaw's contention with regard to Shakespeare, that the first consideration was the music of the verse.

It annoyed him to see excesses of realistic and naturalistic business in Shakespearean productions. In all poetic dramas the first essential was rhythm. It was necessary, of course, to be reasonable in the matter of rhythm, emotion can, upon rare occasions, displace it, but metre was not rhythm, and there were various forms of rhythm, various times at which the throb of the drama should proceed. Literature was not the first thing in the theatre, whatever critics might say. The main thing that people came to see was human nature. The passion in some of the older plays of modern times was an asset. He referred to " The Second Mrs Tanqueray " and to Miss Gladys Cooper's unrestrained, picturesque, and passionate handling of Pinero's heroine, and pointed out that it was drawing all London primarily because it was a piece of acting, that the actress had unselfishly hidden her own personality and given a vital piece of acting.

Mr Dean has published in full the lecture given at the Theatre Exhibition. It is too long for me to refer to in detail, but a few extracts may be possible here. He referred to the work of Mr Norman Bel Geddes, a young American artist, some of whose designs are on view in the exhibition. Mr Geddes had imagined and drawn plans for a theatre with no proscenium at all. The stage is a vast arena in one corner of a square building, with seats in a large semi-circle all around it. A huge dome forms the background to the whole. When this dome is illuminated it envelops the audience in the same light as the drama, thus helping them to merge themselves entirely in the play. The stage can be rapidly sunk to the cellar level on a huge lift, big changes of scene being effected in a few minutes of darkness.

Here are Mr Dean's observations upon electric light, which he describes as an inestimable gift to the theatre :—

" Have you ever reflected upon the tremendous emotional quality of light ? What instinct is it that makes you draw the curtains on a frosty winter's night, switch off the light, and draw near the bright embers ? You watch the dancing

shadows on the wall in silence, until an emotional
state is induced in you quite unconsciously.
Now is the time to sweep away misunderstandings,
to recall past memories, perhaps to sing old songs.
Such is the mysterious, comforting light of the
fireside. A tremendous and most precious gift
has been put into our hands and as yet we are
scarcely awake to the fact. I go so far as to say
that the future of decoration, I do not say design,
lies wholly with the electrician. The painter
must look to his laurels. Soon he must go back
to the studio where he properly belongs. It is
in this emotional quality of light, this power to
blend in with and to vivify the emotional state
created by the drama without any intrusion of
detail, that the most powerful instrument of
stage decoration lies.

" As yet we mostly use light realistically.
Eventually it will have to be used decoratively
and to illustrate and magnify emotion. It is
in this swift and clear recognition of this fact
as much as by the beauty of his design that
Adolphe Appia has justified his title to be the
greatest of all the workers in the new stagecraft. Appia contends that it is an insufficient
reform to substitute three-dimensional scenery

for the old-fashioned two-dimensional stuff, not enough to substitute papier mâché rocks for those painted on the back drop.   With the living actor placed against such things one can easily detect the fraud.   Instead he has sought to weld the background into harmony with the living actor by the use of the only other vital force available in the theatre, namely, light. Somewhere, in speaking of the forest of Siegfried, he says : ' We must no longer try to create the illusion of a forest ; but instead the illusion of a man in the atmosphere of a forest.   When the forest trees, stirred by the breeze, attract the attention of Siegfried, we, the spectators, should see Siegfried bathed in the moving lights and shadows and not the movements of rags of canvas agitated by stage tricks.   The scenic illusion lies in the living presence of the actor.' Appia's theories that in light we have the only force capable of holding the scene painter and designer in necessary subjection to the actor, that in light lies the one motive power capable of forcing inanimate things into a living contribution to the human emotion, were, of course, at the time they were first formulated, quite revolutionary.   I have always thought that he was an even greater apostle than Craig of the god whose name is Dionysius. It is Appia whom I wish to follow."

Dealing with the question of acting Mr Dean stated that what we need more urgently than anything else is the return of the actor to the theatre.

" The indifferent state of acting is keeping the theatres of London empty just as much as is commercialism. Let there be a generation of great actors once more, and your theatres will be thronged, your dramatists will awaken and will write new and even greater plays. Drama began with the actor; it will finish with the actor.

" The dramatist is as much to blame as the artist, and more so, for he knew better. Let me remind you that I refer to the English-speaking stage. Instead of encouraging the actor to create character, he has insisted upon casting his plays round the physical attributes and personal idiosyncrasies of a few well-known players. The thing began with Pinero; and it has gone on ever since."

Mr Dean expresses the opinion that the most inartistic stage in the world is the American stage. " Here," says he, " you have Trades Unionism rampant, the relations between actor, audience, and manager thoroughly unsatisfactory, the worst evils of commercialism visible everywhere, with a delicious fungus known as the play-doctor busily engaged in warping and twisting other people's work to suit the demands of star performers. Nothing," concluded Mr Dean, " can kill the drama. It is engrained in the heart of man. It is better than cinemas, jazz bands, and all the contrivances of distraction. It is man himself. Let the actor arise then, put on the mantle of Roscius, and act to the very limits of his soul. Let Language, Form, Colour, and Light be his humble servants."

XXII

STAGE DIALOGUE

NOTHING appears easier to the average beginner in dramatic composition than the writing of fluent dialogue. The facility with which natural characteristic patter seems to flow from one's pen is little short of phenomenal. The resultant product, however, when analysed, alas, proves horrifying, if not to the author, to all those upon whom it is inflicted.

The crackle of stage conversation seems so simple to kindle, seems so readily maintainable, so quick to burst into a blaze of furious verbal conflict that page follows page with voluminous ferocity, and before he can say " Jack Robinson " our tyro has produced a four-act play full of nothing but endless, aimless, flippant, and tedious conversations.

I know of only one dramatic author with sufficient mental vigour, sufficient verbal dexterity, sufficient originality of outlook to be able to attempt and achieve success solely upon dialogue. He was, and is, the most acute critic our stage has known, and he is the only living playwright whose works are equally popular in all the highly civilised countries of the world. If Mr Bernard Shaw's success in that little tilled field of the conversational play should tempt our newer authors into following his plough, I hope others may be given the task of reviewing their efforts, for of all tedious duties that of criticising the " talky " play is one of the most exasperating.

First-nighters have recently had to endure several curious examples of over-epigrammatic work from novices, not all of them without promise, but cases where the blue pencil of the producer might have been exercised with salutary effect before the curtain rose. The young author must beware of letting loose the flood of volubility—otherwise he may drown his play and his own chances of success in the flood of talk. He must not busy himself creating cascades and fanciful jets of chatter to prove what a sparkling and brilliant writer like himself can do with stage dialogue. The epigram that is forced is worse than a damp squib. It not only fails to explode. It causes offence.

Dialogue should be the inevitable product of two parents : the character and the situation. It is the flame that, sparkling around the author's ideas, sends them smouldering to failure or blazing to success.

We cannot ask of the author that he shall attempt to reproduce in all their hideous, barbaric actuality the trivial chatterings, the apeish blither of everyday conversation. Were he to attempt a record of the disconnected, abbreviated slurrings and mumblings of real speech, he would be accused of caricature, and damned for an outrageous burlesque. Were he to demand of his players the amazing breaking up of sentences, of words, the ejaculations, the distorted moanings and whinings, the unfinished endings, the mispronunciations, the commingling of utterances, and the rude interjectionary onslaughts of our modern drawing-room babel, he would be charged with insanity or something worse.

But we can ask of him that he should adopt one of two courses. We can expect him to make his characters express their own individuality respectively, or, *per contra*, be an outlet for his own thought and personality, if they be sufficiently entertaining. The former method is, of course, the more artistic, but some of our most successful dramatic authors have secured their fame upon the latter basis. The comedy in which each character has something really witty or amusing to say is readily pardoned, and may be exalted into a classic before its author dies. The circumstance that it is an unnatural exaltation of the art of conversation may prove an asset and not a defect. We have, on the other hand, several modern writers—notably Mr Galsworthy and Mr Arnold Bennett—whose characters observe a conscientious regard for nature and truth, and seldom or never make a remark that sounds improbable or artificial coming from their lips. We do not hear the author's voice, but those of his personages.

Yet what a little while it is since the actors had something they could dig their teeth into, and gloried in giving utterance to the most stilted, prolix, and artificial of speeches! The dialogue of the Jacobean stage was difficult to negotiate; the dialogue of the early Victorian drama before the days of Tom Robertson was a fearsome and wonderful thing; yet both types were not without charm and beauty. The knack of brilliant repartee in comedy seems to have been specialised in by Irishmen. Sheridan leaps triumphantly to the eyes as the first great exponent of wit in dialogue. In later days Wilde has had no superior in the neat reply, the smartness of which makes us forget its utter unsuitability to the character supposed to be giving it birth. Gilbert's dialogue always had a quality peculiarly his own. It was generally ironic, mostly legal in its precision and logical turns. It seldom took any cognisance of its stage parentage and betrayed the author in every sentence.

I doubt whether Barrie has any specially detectable flavour in his dialogue. His marked individuality finds an outlet in the idea rather than in its method of verbal expression. The earlier comedies of Somerset Maugham were memorable for their dependence upon wit and the *bon mot*. His remarkable play " The Circle " was furnished with most amusing debates, but each remark seemed appropriate to the character. Mr Milne is one of our ablest writers of fascinating conversation. He can seldom resist a touch of humour in each retort.

There are some of us who sigh for the modern author who will restore to our English stage the difficulties of blank verse. There are many amongst us who contend that the chief object of the stage is to improve, our speech, not to degrade it, to show the public how melodious, how enchanting, how inspiring, how noble the English speech can sound when perfectly delivered by trained actors and actresses, free from pedantry, yet revelling in accuracy, and who despise the mimicry and debasement of speech popular to-day—not only round our dining tables, but in our theatres.

The truth is, there is something to be said for both sides. We cannot do without our natural dialogue, our satirical but truthful reflections of faults and slovenliness of the tongue we practise. Neither should we fail to cultivate that purer, gentler, and beautiful habit of talk through which the high idea can find an idealised and exquisite expression.

XXIII

" OLD LAMPS AND NEW "

WITH Sir Squire Bancroft's retirement from management in 1885, the theatre lost an asset which it has never been quite able to replace. Future historians of the English stage will probably regard the Bancrofts as the founders and originators of the modern so-called " natural " or " reserved " school of acting. It would not be true, perhaps, to say that they " discovered " Tom Robertson, but they were the first management to back Robertson's ideas and substitute plays with natural characters speaking natural dialogue amidst actual surroundings, and handling actual properties, plays in which a real attempt was made to hold the mirror up to nature.

The modern stage is, therefore, under an unredeemable debt to this man, who, with tremendous courage and more than ordinary perspicacity, detected and eradicated all the weaknesses and errors of the old-time school of acting, with its mouthing, its artificial heroics, its long speeches, specially designed to give the actor " something to dig his teeth into," its general fustian and rhodomontade, and substituted for it a delicate and accurate reproduction of life.

It may be that if we could to-day transport ourselves by means of some magical Arabian carpet back to those old days of " The Dust-hole " off the Tottenham Court Road, and witness once again performances of " Caste," " School," " Ours," and " Society," we should think them hopelessly old-fashioned. But on the other hand we might not.

In either case there can be no question that Sir Squire and his wife were responsible for as revolutionary a train of thought in the theatre as has ever been set in motion by a single management.

Apart from the improvement they un-doubtedly caused in the methods of the actor, it is to them that we owe the modern luxurious stall, for in order to meet the cost of their beautiful and expensive productions they had to resort to higher prices, which the public, in view of the value given, gladly paid.

Whilst, however, theatre-goers have every reason to be grateful to the Bancrofts, their success, unfortunately, brought into existence a host of inferior imitators, and it is to their charlatan successors that much of the modern ineffectiveness of characterisation and indistinctness of delivery on the stage must be ascribed.

These people have always lost sight of the fact that the great thing on the stage is not to *be* natural, but to *appear* natural. All theatrical art requires to pass through the mould of technique. The technique may and must vary according to the temperament of the artist and his capacity, but the most successful artist will be the one who succeeds in creating a sense of illusion, who makes you forget your surroundings and the fact that you are in the theatre rather than the one who solely evokes comment by the naturalness and truthfulness of his art. There must be ideality in acting. Sir Squire Bancroft and his wife had the good fortune to be trained in a school where ideality was paramount, and where clearness of enunciation and the necessity of being heard by the man in the back of the gallery were always prime considerations. Therefore, however natural their acting might appear, their speech was always audible, their emotions and their actions well regulated.

How much or how little attention is paid to elocution or clearness of speech on the stage to-day can be discovered by a visit to our principal theatres. " The age of declamation is past," said a friend of mine when I broached this subject to him, but it is scarcely a question of declamatory effort. Take such an actor as Fred Terry, for instance : how consummately natural he always is, yet every word rings out clear and true, and his elocution is invariably a delight to the ear.

XXIV

CONRAD AND THE CRITICS

It has become the custom when plays fail nowadays to blame the critics. Even the critics are commencing to blame each other for the stage failures they see strewn around. So what shall the public believe? Personally I cannot flatter myself that anything I have written ever had the slightest effect upon the fate of any play or player. I think we do not live in times when dramatic journalism is taken seriously. The public prefers to form its own opinion; theatrical criticism at its best or worst is only one man's point of view.

The critic should of course be subjected to the same severity of test as he administers to others. He must not fear or avoid blunt, open criticism of himself or his attitude. And the critic must not exalt himself by allowing others to magnify his own importance; critics as such have very little influence upon the box-office.

The worst of plays often succeed in spite of the critics' wholesale condemnation. The play that they commend and value often drifts into a state that is worse than death, an atrophy that refuses to tell the manager whether success or failure is its lot. These are the deadliest of all pieces, for they induce a prolonged expenditure upon an uncertainty, and in the long run involve their unfortunate proprietor in more loss than a declared and immediate frost.

We are now faced by a new argument on behalf of the unsuccessful playwright. I am told by one of my most respected fellow craftsmen that when such a man as Mr Joseph Conrad, a distinguished novelist, enters the field of drama, I must not " frighten " him from the theatre. I must not speak of his play openly and candidly as a bad bit of work if I think it so, and I am cynically reminded that it is not " a minor crime " for a novelist to fail to understand the limitations of a stage play. My friend Mr Baughan forgets that I can purchase one of Mr Conrad's books for a shilling. If I do not like it, I am at liberty to throw it away and even to jump on it if it annoys me. If I am a playgoer, I cannot, except at the risk of being

considered a rude and boorish fellow, leave the
theatre before the play is over. I have taken
my wife and friend with me. I must listen,
having paid twelve shillings for a stall (perhaps),
willy-nilly to long conversations that have no
bearing on the real story, watch incidents that
strike me as ludicrous without being able to
express my contempt for them, and fill myself
with regrets at the wasted labour of a genius
in pursuing some strange animal whose habits
and traits he has not sufficiently studied or
experienced.

Now, Mr Conrad is much too sensible and
sympathetic a man to tilt at the critics
himself. I should imagine he has as much
philosophy over such an unimportant first
failure as that of " The Secret Agent " as
Goldsmith had over the non-popularity of " The
Good-Natured Man." One-half of the company
were allowed to act in a realistic way, the other
half in a baldly melodramatic key. Some of
the artists drifted from one note to the other.
That Mr Conrad achieved any result at all in
face of this handicap must be put to his credit.
The critics were not responsible for it.

The Theatre must throw its doors open to

all men of brains, but it must not have two standards of criticism where such work as " The Secret Agent " is affected by its judgments. A play is a play, and a novel a novel, and it does not matter by whom the play is written, whether by the most distinguished novelist, or by an ignorant coal-heaver : if it is a bad play the critics must say so, and if it is a good one, they must have a similar dispassionate disinterest in the personality of its authorship. It is the play that matters, not the author.

XXV

" OTHELLO "

" OTHELLO " is one of the sublimest and, at the
same time, the most absurd of tragedies. If in
modern-day life a distinguished African negro
were secretly to woo and marry a delicately
nurtured, fair-complexioned daughter of an
English Cabinet Minister of noble birth, Society
as at present constituted would privately profess
to be terribly shocked, and the popular Press
would devote pages to descriptions and pictures
of the happy pair. Imagine the match to be
publicly disapproved of by the father of the
bride, and subsequently ended in the murder
of the girl by the negro after his translation to
the Governorship of a Crown Colony. Imagine,
also, that the murder is brought about through
jealousy of a preposterous nature at an imaginary
deception invented by the negro's aide-de-camp.
Should we not—all of us—whatever the felicity
or magniloquence of the " journalese " indulged in

to describe these amazing happenings, consider the tragedy as a sorry, sordid and unpleasant affair ? Not one of the participants would be entitled to the smallest pity or sympathy.

Now a magician known as Shakespeare takes a corresponding set of characters and circumstances, and by the wizardry of his words and fancy converts it into one of the most wonderful romances the world is ever likely to know. From a ridiculous tangle of bloody and incredible stupidities he evolves a splendid story that has been transported with success into every known language on earth, and that will probably last as long as the terms drama and tragedy have the smallest significance for playgoers.

" To be wroth with one we love doth work like madness in the brain."

When Coleridge wrote these words he had, so far as we can tell, no thoughts of Othello in the back of his mind, but it is quite possible that he had, for the anger of Othello with Desdemona is the nearest approach to madness any intelligent man (even a great General) has ever displayed, and, as has been said so many times before, it was " all about a pocket-handkerchief."

It is undesirable to play Othello as a mad-

man, though I have seen him so represented on
the stage, and it follows that the fury, the
epileptic raging, and the storm of Othello's
passion of jealousy and distrust are always
difficult to make convincing. The Othello has
to depend not only upon himself, but upon his
Iago. The actor who undertakes the part of
the Moor must have an unusual range of qualities
—he must have nobility, simplicity, brutality,
tenderness, dignity, pathos, intellectuality and
a sense of poetry. The slightest touch of in-
sincerity, bluster, or conceit, and your Othello
is doomed. It is easy to make Othello a ranting
blubberer. It is easy to overact him, and even
Salvini has been accused by no less a critic than
Lewes of this fault.

When Mr Fagan staged " Othello " at the
Court in April 1921, Mr Godfrey Tearle was the
Othello. He satisfied me to a reasonable degree
in every one of the essential requirements of the
part and still was able to refute successfully any
criticism upon the score of exaggeration. This
is not to say that Mr Tearle was perfect in the
character. It would be ridiculous to say so.
But I imagine it will be a long time before the
present generation of playgoers will be able

again to see a representation of the part so full of charm, grandeur, music and passion as the Othello of Mr Tearle. His performance was full of little redeeming touches intended by the actor to alleviate the bestiality and brutality suggested by the lines. When, for instance, he has to propose that Emilia should become a spy upon her mistress this man shrinks from himself with horror almost as quickly as the thought enters his mind. He was slower to suspect than most Othellos, and only reached the extreme of violence when the situation made it compulsory. In certain of the earlier passages I thought him mawkish and monotonous. His address to the Senate was musically delivered, but for me did not carry conviction. He had, I thought, the right degree of gradation in his tempo and energy, and the outburst against Iago in the middle of the play was magnificently done. His rich voice and sincerity of address filled me with admiration, whilst his incoherent and inarticulate convulsions of wrath thrilled me by their sheer savagery and absence of control.

It is all very well to complain of this hysterical form of acting as overstrung, and to call for its repression, but the character of Othello is

throughout a contest between gentility and
animalism. In that combat the latter has a
brief triumph, ultimately atoned for by a superb
suicide. There was nothing in Mr Tearle's
Othello of the wretched self-pity that so frequently discredits the character. It is distinctly
an Othello to be seen.

As for the Iago, I will not commit the impertinence of disputing Mr Rathbone's method
of playing this king of villains. He can be
acted, as I have said before, in a thousand and
one ways. Mr Rathbone's method was as good
if not a little bit better than many others. This
Iago is an intellectual demon, a brainy, subtle,
insinuating scamp who might very well deceive
a shrewder judge of human nature than the
Moor. He was a trifle too nasal in his intona-
tions, but his youthfulness, his zest in plotting,
his fantastic malignancy, and the contrast made
by the latter with his natural assumption of
" honesty," were of tremendous assistance in
all the duets with Othello, and particularly were
they valuable in the soliloquies in which he
reveals the damnable depths of his turpitude.
There was a superciliousness, a sneering contempt for the Cassio and the Roderigo, whilst

there was something of terror and dread suggested in his hatred of the Moor. He was the
most poetic Iago I can remember, and suggested
that in his leisure hours the Ancient was something of an æsthete.

And now I come to a consideration of the
Desdemona and the Emilia. I have always
thought that Emilia is by far the better acting
part of the two. It is true that she has very
little to do until the last act, but in that act the
waiting-woman has opportunities of showing her
capacity for a tragic outburst denied to the
Desdemona. The latter lady is a heroine a
little out of key with modern ideas of woman-
hood. Any woman who can calmly hear herself
called " whore " and " strumpet " and other
polite epithets of that nature, and still maintain
an attitude of affectionate obedience to the
gentleman guilty of such a sad breach of
courtesy to his wife, can make small appeal to
the minds of present-day audiences. In the
days when wives, if they did not do as their
husbands wanted them to, were beaten, Desdemona no doubt would be considered an amiable
and desirable companion, but the modern actress
who has to play Desdemona labours under very

considerable handicaps. She has to make charm out of insipidity. She has to create beauty out of helplessness and sublimity out of despair, pathos out of stupidity, and depict a dog-like devotion to a coloured man as an idealistic and wholly admirable feeling. If I were a " star " actress I should absolutely decline to play Desdemona, whatever salary I was offered. I should much prefer to act in a modern bedroom play with the whole of my back exposed to the audience, provided I could have an opportunity of saying some home truths to the modern husband and letting him see that married life was a partnership and not a matter of slavery.

Miss Madge Titheradge did as well as any actress can be expected to do with such an ineffective and depressing bundle of suppressed self and will. Her emotional capabilities are considerable, and if her wig were not so obviously false and flaxen she might easily have run in fit double harness with the Othello. As it was, she suggested a musical comedy actress who had, like the heroine of " Romance," determined to be good in spite of her past—a sort of Shake-spearean " Belle of New York " without the accent.

XXVI

OUR THREE-QUARTER STAGE

OUR actors and play-producers, nearly all of them, are afflicted with the three-quarter palsy. I know not how else to describe the tradition, the habit, the convention, the accursed paralysis of movement they affect. Have you never noticed that it is impossible for most actors to avoid walking and talking with their faces almost wholly turned to their audiences, that nearly all the characters in every scene have at least three-quarters of their faces turned towards you, that they even cross the stage three-quarter fashion, that the chairs and sofas on our stages are mostly arranged three-quarters facing you, whilst some of our finest actresses impudently glare over the footlights with their full faces up into the gallery, as though to say, " Look at me ; I am the star paid to shine at a salary of £200 a week with extras for matinées."

I often wonder why this ludicrously unnatural

tradition, which must be stultifying to any
conscientious, clear-thinking artist, has been
allowed to overpower that freedom of motion,
that disregard for the spectator without which
art becomes as simple slavery and stupidity as
the wearing of boots that hurt and cramp the
feet. Our actors should look into this. Instead
of holding the mirror up to nature, they are
holding themselves, as it were, spiritually up
to a mirror. It is as if they were always slyly
seeking to see themselves in the glass and show
themselves off like spoilt children.

In farce, direct acknowledgment of one's
audience is not only permissible but essential.
The comic actor of the lower class may give
himself such freedom with his spectators as
cannot be tolerated in the comedian of refinement and distinction. In drama or tragedy I
think the most sorrowful incidents are those
that occur after the end of each act, when the
performers bow and scrape to the audience and
to each other, forgetful of the fact that such
distractions are impertinences, rude breaches
of illusion, and insults to the author. Deliberate
avoidance of the audience is equally culpable.
If you are a real actress, there is only one thing

to do with the man who has paid his money to see you. Strive to make him think you haven't noticed him. Man-like, he will immediately become interested in you.

But illusion is the great thing. In that one word " illusion "—the illusion of time, place, atmosphere and passion—we have the open sesame of the whole theatre. To take us out of ourselves, to make us forget, to deceive us, to capture the senses—what more precious power can the actor wield? Yet how seldom is illusion genuinely deceptive and creative illusion striven for. The sky drop cloths, the built-up scenery that seldom fits, the smell of sized cloth and timber, the raked stage floor, the wings, the horribly set and framelike proscenium, the boxes, the footlights—all contribute to the overpowering effect of artificiality and loss of illusion. The illustrated peeps into the actor's private life, the gossiper's dives behind the scenes—all these are huge mistakes in art. One does not need to be high-browed to realise that.

I blame the present proscenium for much of our troubles. We shall never progress till we abandon it. It reminds us of and preserves our

theatrical limitations.   What can one hope for
shut behind a frame?   We at once think of
paint, and paint never speaks, though it may
stink. The De Courville joy-plank may seem
to some abominable, and in the flagrant in-
timacy it establishes between actress and public
it is perhaps regrettable, but there is light
somewhere in that direction, as Reinhardt and
the ancient Greeks long before him discovered
to their advantage.   Or must we push our
scenes further back, telescopic fashion?   Mr
Asche and Mr Barker, Mr Knoblock, Mr
Hackett, and others have experimented to
good purpose in this direction—retrograde, I
think, only in one sense.   In any event, we
cannot allow this three-quarter craze to continue.   Abolish the proscenium, and it will at
once meet the fate it deserves.

XXVII

SOME REFLECTIONS UPON ACTING

NOTHING matters so much in an actor as manners. As Emerson once said, there is always a best way of doing everything, if it be only to boil an egg, and manners are the happy ways of doing things. By his manners must we judge the actor. By his manners the managers reject or select him for certain parts. He must be an expert in bad manners as well as good ones. The secret of success in many an actor has been his form, his behaviour, his deportment.

Too many players are obsessed with themselves. They study their own lines through and through. They concentrate upon their own parts and speeches to the exclusion of the other characters and the other lines in the play. They have no eyes for the people to whom they are supposed to speak. They converse with themselves, sometimes to themselves, sometimes to the audience. The best actor knows the parts of others as thoroughly as he does his own. He knows that a knowledge of the play and a consideration of what the other characters are thinking are essential to an understanding of his duties.

.   .   .   .   .

Yet must the actor know himself, his gestures, his expressions, facial and physical, his equipment through and through. He must have complete control over the machine. He must discover his weaknesses and correct them one by one laboriously without appearing to labour in doing so. He must discover his strength and develop it to the point of perfection. If he be gifted with a beautiful voice, he must not become too sensible of its beauty, nor allow it to be impaired through an independent reliance upon its attraction.

The eye is as useful to the actor as his voice. Both can speak eloquently. Both can be dumb. Both can be overworked. The eye of the actor is as a rule the most restless of organs. It roves persistently audiencewards. It contradicts the utterance, or at least refuses to give it support. Some actors roll their eyes like a ship crossing the Channel, others are notorious for blinking. Some keep them half-shut all the while they act, opening them only in their dressing-rooms ; others have no power of eye movement or expression. Glass eyes would be just as helpful as theirs.

The hands are the least controllable. At any rate, beginners in acting generally fail properly to control them. The proper thing is to forget them and let them do naturally just what they wish to do. Which is difficult.

.   .   .   .   .

Confidence is a fine thing in an actor, yet I find a greater charm in the nervous diffidence of an artist approaching his task with a sense of its danger and importance. There is as much fascination for me in the exalted, watchful, timorous attitude of the modest player as in the glib, easy, pushful certainty of the self-satisfied smirker assured of your favour before he asks it.

We must not, however, despise the vain actor. Vanity and good acting are frequently inseparable. Vanity has been a stimulus to some of the finest of temperamental performers. A little praise has inspired many a great performance.

. . . . .

I was amused the other day to note that a well-known man of the theatres was decrying the art of acting and declaring emphatically that there was no such thing as " great " acting. There is certainly little " great " acting to-day, but to say that the giants of the past were all myths is the veriest moonshine.

I have seen a few real " giants " in my time —actors and actresses whom I have no hesitation in pronouncing great artists. They were great because they took a " great " view of their responsibilities. They were great because they despised everything that was mean, base, or trivial in their art, and because they aspired to perfection even if they did not always attain it. Great harm has been done to the cause of " great " acting by the latter-day booming of conscientiousness and exaltation of all-round painstaking mediocrity. The necessity of good team work has been unduly praised at the expense of individual excellence. I like to see the company play well together. No one appreciates the give and take of comradeship on the stage more than I, but when it comes to choosing between " great " acting and team work, I plump for the former every time.

The star system has its drawbacks, but at least it gets people out of a rut. Acting is not a democratic art. It needs the supremacy of individualism, or it will assuredly perish.

XXVIII

THE WORLD'S MONSTER PLAYHOUSE

HAVE you ever ridden a nightmare to death? Have you ever felt yourself falling, falling into countless black pits or abysses, sideless and bottomless? Have strange, incomprehensible noises in the night thrilled your drowsing nerves —failed to awake you, but disturbed your rest? Have the sensations of a De Quincey as an opium-eater been yours? Have you watched in your dreams myriads of long-robed figures striding ever onwards; listened to thousands of voices as of lost souls whispering, weeping, murmuring, crying, shouting, shrieking, bellowing into a Babel of sound? Have you gazed in dumb bewilderment, as if half-blinded, whilst gross, unshapely masses of form moved slowly, silently, surely in the dark into coherent outline, whilst human hands and arms by the million stretched upwards to the Gods that laugh ?

What are those trumpetings, that music, that tramp of feet ? What is that thin ray of light that feebly trickles from the heavens ? See ! It extends itself into a shaft—a beam. It grows in radiance—then a burst of sunshine—the blazing fires of a desert sun reveals the living scene—faces and figures, clearer and clearer, come from the mists—old friends, familiar characters in well-known clothes. They talk in strange, uncouth and guttural note. Herr Gott ! I am in Germany—these men are ancient Romans. There is Mark Antony, Brutus and Cassius, Casca, and the rest, and there is Julius the mighty. This is no vision. It is merely Reinhardt's Grossespielhaus at Berlin, and the play is " Julius Cæsar." No ! My friends, I have not taken leave of my senses. I am merely trying to convey to you the mental effect the production and the theatre have upon me. It was a phantasmagoria. Had I never seen it I could not have believed it.

Who in these days would wish to be classed amongst those idiots who praise the achievements of every country but their own ? On the other hand, who shall deny that other lands have much to show and much to teach us? Who, also, shall say that nationality—that singular product of climate, soil and racial mixture—does not affect results in art, especially the art of the theatre? The German of the past had great ambitions. The German of to-day is still soaring in the clouds. Nothing can be too huge, too colossal, too tremendous for him. Even his monuments are always massive, often clumsy from their size, ludicrous in their hugeness, like giants bursting into tears.

This craze for the gross has found an advocate in Germany's most famous theatrical producer, Herr Max Reinhardt. He has turned a Berlin circus just off the Karlstrasse into one of the vastest, most amazing, and mysterious theatres in the world. Its entrances, exits, and corridors constitute a labyrinth. It seats five thousand people, and on the night of my visit it was absolutely packed. To secure my stall I had to stand at ten o'clock in the morning for half an hour in a queue of people, many of them munching food Berliner fashion.

The impression this mammoth playhouse gave me from the exterior was that of some gigantic pagan mausoleum. It is hideously red in colour, with sloping roofs like a South Sea temple, simple in style, panelled with big, upturned pendules, parallel and graduated — with the obvious intention of conveying a sense of multitude and mass. Repetition is the keynote of its architecture—repetition of shape, object and colour. The consequences are consequently unforgettable. The same plan prevails inside and out. The interior, with its sea of faces, staggers and dazes. From the circular roof stiffly hang hundreds of stalactites, regular in form, drooping again in pendule style systematically from the cavernous and ringed ceiling. No lights are visible, and the place, dimly lit like some cathedral, provokes a hush as one enters. At the same time it arouses no pleasurable sensations—rather the reverse. It stuns. It is like some freakish habitation of a German gnome, whose insanity has driven him to think colossally. We are hypnotised, confused by the force, the size, the repetition of the conception, but there is no beauty, no grace, no felicity of construction—merely the grotesque and the gigantic.

As one might expect, its arena-like shape

arouses expectations of equestrian exploits, zoological spectacle, and falling clowns. The stage seemed to me more than five times wider than that of Drury Lane. The action takes place, however, quite as much in the apron-like pit or arena as on the stage proper. There are no rising and falling of curtains, no sudden putting down of lights and sudden disclosures of a lighted scene. The scenes seem to grow, to evolve themselves out of blackness, and each break in the action provokes the nightmare-like sensations previously described. The persons in the play seem to come out of the ground in front of the stage.

No words at my command can convey the sublimity yet monstrousness of the whole idea, production as well as theatre. The German worship of Shakespeare is well known. It is not to be admitted, however, that their knowledge of his works is equal to their veneration for him as a writer. I prefer Reinhardt's pre-war work on a smaller stage. True, he is able to give you those Gustave Doré-like effects —his masterly control of crowds stands him in good stead in such a big house as this, but what can any theatrical *metteur-en-scène*, however brilliant, do with a stage where the actor has always to shout his lines, and where he must run half a mile to make an exit? Poor Lucius, sent by Brutus here and there, seemed to me to be constantly sprinting. The leg muscles of the players will be finely developed after six months' practice in such pedestrianism.

I have spoken of the crowds. They were perhaps at times a trifle too docile, but the Forum scene was astonishingly well done, and here the shouting and strident vocalisation of the actors did not seem so discordant. At other times it required great elocutionary ability to avoid a sense of labour and mechanical energy grinding out words to make them reach the distant ear. The two ladies of the company were the chief sufferers. Yet I must say that I think these German players did much better under the difficulties of the large auditorium than would most of our English actors. They are never afraid of making themselves heard.

All the actors adopt the fustian roaring methods, digging their teeth into the lines. The Cassius was the strangest and most full-blooded Cassius I have ever seen. He surpassed Franklin McLeay for vigour and ferocity. There was little of the lean and hungry man about him. He was played as a very tall young man, full of dash, vigour, and stomach. The Brutus was fatly philosophical, but quietly forcible, in pleasing contrast to the Cassius, who seemed to try to make up in noise all that he wanted in power.

The quarrel scene seemed to me atrociously done. It was just a trial of lung-power, each man bellowing at the other for all he was worth, like a couple of ill-tempered sergeants in the army. The Julius Cæsar held his head in the air and indulged in hieratical attitudes, attempting to impart to the character a Teutonic dignity that resembled a full balloon just ready to burst. When he died it took him about twenty minutes to fall, from the rostrum on which he was perched, down the steps in the arena, where he curled himself up neatly like a cat before the hearth. This scene, generally so theatrically impressive, struck me as merely comical and disappointing.

The Mark Antony I liked better than any of the others. Although he was repulsively obese, and lumbered rather than walked, he had a greater command over his emotions, his voice, and his gestures than the rest, and better than one expects from a Continental actor. His lament over Cæsar's dead body was, despite his unattractive physique, most pathetic and impressive. His handling of the speech to the mob was brilliant in its gradual, crafty, and cumulative intensity, ending with an outburst irresistible in its spontaneity.

XXIX

WANTED—NEW ART FORMS

" THE DRAMA'S LAWS "

DISCUSSING the stage with a young friend of mine the other day, I raised a point which seemed to excite his interest and may be worth touching upon in this column. I was commenting upon the conventionalism of the average playwright, his regard for what are generally called the rules of construction; his respect, barbaric in its intensity, for tradition and technique as practised by our forerunners. There is no doubt we are stifling our progress by blind acceptance of the old laws. We have a proscenium that destroys naturalism; auditoria that assist neither sight nor hearing; a school of actors and actresses afraid to speak out and make themselves heard; a system of changing scenes as archaic as the Egyptian method of drawing water from a well —hardly one revolving or ascending stage in our whole country; and yet we expect innovations from our dramatists and audacity from our managers. True, we get the latter (sometimes), but it is the wrong sort of audacity. It resembles the thing colloquially known as " cheek."

The playwright has unfortunately to work not to please himself but to please others. Therein lies the secret of his failure. The painter of pictures can in his leisure hour amuse himself by following experimental lines for his own pleasure; the musician can burst into fresh harmonies unfettered by the knowledge that unless the result gratifies and satisfies or interests someone beside himself his work has no existence at all; it can have no being. The co-operation of other minds is essential to the playwright. He must depend not only upon his producer, his manager, his artists, his actors, his wig-makers, his property masters, his call-boys, his lighting experts, his bill-posters, and his publicity men (or women); he has also to rely upon his audience, for the fate of each play varies in accordance with the audience before whom it is presented. " The drama's laws, etc.," I must not overwork the old quotation. It applies to dramatic authors even more than to actors.

What would be thought of a dramatist who,

instead of eliminating from his dialogue, as is our stage custom, all the flotsam and jetsam of everyday conversation, carefully loaded it, accurately and naturally, with all those interruptions of thought and action that Nature, bless her, always insists upon?

However placid our lives may be, each of us must at some time or another have suffered a real scene in them. We have been strung up into a passion. Eloquence has poured itself unchecked from someone else upon our heads— Or we have thrown out the wrath of the moment upon theirs. Have these scenes gone with the swiftness, the certainty, the concentration, the finish of a play by a Pinero, a Jones, a Maugham, or a Bennett? However lifelike these crises in our comedies, have they the smallest resemblance to that one scene in which you yourself were the great participant? Wherein lies the difference? That way progress lies.

The acid test of playwriting, as of acting, is sincerity. The object of the theatre is primarily entertainment, but its greatest aim is, or should be, to hold up the mirror—and to be sure that the mirror has no convex or concave surface, but is exact and true.

Your skilled, notorious producer must have his climax just so. It must come just in the " right " place. He forgets that the greatest drama comes in a trifle—the most poignant moment is an accident, the most amusing incident is an improvisation. We cannot order art about like a nurserymaid. Discipline, so valuable in the field, is something to be feared in the theatre.

Take your play to a manager. If it is not built in accordance with his ideas of construction, if it is not what he will style a well-constructed play, what hope have you ? Or suppose he is of that rare breed of director, the man who has no regard for the well-made piece, and he asks you for the moral or the motive of your play, will it avail you to answer him—Life has no moral ; there is no motive in ninety-nine per cent. of men's lives ?

I make a plea for less circumspectness of direction in playwriting—a plea for the intro-duction of the apparently irrelevant—after the fashion of Nature. A man cannot always be shaking hands with the long arm of coincidence. Even Shaw in " You Never Can Tell " burdens his tale with strange coincidences. It may be argued that it is just these coincidences that make the piece dramatic, that unless the tale is told concisely and without trappings it will seem diffuse, rambling and incoherent. Well, he must judge our story and deal with it accordingly.

I love Tchehov, the Russian, and his way of interpolating oddly into the fabric of his dreams so many facts and figures that seem to have no bearing upon his argument. They have all of them a considered significance, and it will be apparent to you if you too will use your thinking-box, but these orderly, neat and machine-made dramas tire the critic far more easily than the spontaneous and unstudied aberrations of a gifted mind.

When we can hear upon the stage dialogue that does not fit its hearer like a glove—or a suit from Conduit Street—when we can see people behaving as erratically and inexplicably as they do in the world of reality, we may be sure we are progressing in the field of higher comedy. Meanwhile I suppose we must be grateful for the many first-class entertainments of the conventional and accepted brand available for our studies.

XXX

THE MUSIC HALL

THERE is an Elizabethan robustness about the
music hall, proving how simple and honest a
people we are, and how much we dislike subtlety
and intricate processes of thought. The mere
mention of beer will always bring a smile, if
not a positive roar. The lodger has still his
uses as a laugh-producer. Marital infidelity is
as safe a card as it is in the legitimate drama.
When the fun flags, hit the other fellow on
the head or prod him in the pit of the stomach.
Trip over yourself and generally play the giddy
goat. These were the recipes of the music-
hall artists of the days of my youth, and
strangely and wonderfully they preserve their
popularity.

Music-hall audiences are notoriously generous.
They seem to me more responsive and demonstrative than theatre audiences, for the
good and sufficient reason that as a rule people

receive better value in the music hall than they do in the theatre. But it is well not to trade too much upon that generosity. I have often found myself bored beyond measure, and brought to the conclusion that the " turns " were trading on their past reputations, and not on their present merits.

A fierce light beats upon the " single turn." It must be exceptionally talented to hold its own. In a play the individual artist receives every kind of assistance in every kind of direction. On the music hall such a performer is compelled to rely upon his own ability and capacity for making good. High animal spirits form the safest passport to the favour of a music-hall audience. Extravagance of method, exuberance of action, breadth and unlimited assurance—these are the things that matter.

Dress up a tiny little gargoyle of a man in a most ridiculous court robe, over which he falls or jumps every second, smother his face with the reddest of red paint, rig him out in a red wig and make him crack the most ancient of chestnuts about the manners and habits of the aristocracy, and you have the " star turn." Supplement his efforts by those of a lady styled

" just a comedienne," who takes the audience into her confidence and engages in a series of amorous confidences with the leader of the orchestra, and you have one of the " hits " of the afternoon.

It has always struck me as curious that the music-hall manager and artist should exhibit a general and uniform distrust of taxing the patience of their audience. The breathless promptitude with which turn follows turn, the hustle of the orchestra, the inevitable accompaniment of a serious performer by some ridiculous personage with his clothes torn to tatters, or with some fiendish or egregious make-up in which his features are transformed into a semblance of a green cheese; these things form factors in the entertainment of the masses which always give me food for regret and surprise. Yet there is really nothing to be surprised at. The audience are simply children of a larger growth who love these freaks and grotesques very much as they used to love their gollywogs in the nursery.

XXXI

SARAH BERNHARDT

WHAT can I say of the great Sarah that has not been said already ? What eloquent, discerning, justifiable tribute of memory can I pay her that has not been rendered already by those who knew her, understood her and loved her better than I did ?

The world has thrown its flowers—perishable and everlasting—at Sarah's feet. The services of the dead have even been called on for the purposes of writing an obituary notice. Column upon column of newspapers all over the world have been filled with eulogy, estimate, record and lamentation on this passing of a great actress. Just valuation, absurd panegyric, common sense and nonsense have vied with each other at her death as in her life. It only remains for me, an insignificant scribe, who has wasted many years of life in pursuit of great acting, to join the funeral throng as one of the many mourners.

I do so with mingled feelings. I recollect
many thrills of excitement, sensations of pleasure,
dramatic joys that the dead woman gave me
in her time. But I cannot obliterate, try as
I will, some painful remembrances, a sense of
hollow mockery at the craft of the stage, its
feverish anxiety for adulation regardless of
truth, and the general neglect of critical responsibility in the face of great reputations.

What has Sarah Bernhardt left behind her
for the younger generation ? Did her method
point the way to a new technique ? Did her
art lighten and make easier the ways of those
who must follow in her footsteps ? We
can say of her at once that she was always a
picturesque personality. She must remain for
thousands a unique and extraordinary theatrical
memory. Capricious to an extreme as a woman,
she carried her caprice into her calling.
She could seldom play the same part for two
nights in succession in the same key. Her
moods had all the inconstancy and the
variety of the sky. I am fond of believing
that the actor's art is imperishable, and
that it is transmitted by observation, training
and unconscious imitation from generation to

generation. Many of Rachel's assets were repeated in Bernhardt. There are echoes of Bernhardt on the Parisian stage to-day, and though the body of the dead actress may rest in the cemetery of Père la Chaise, or in that island off the coast of Brittany, all that she stands for as an actress, all that she meant as the embodiment of a woman, will go on asserting itself through the ages.

Sarah was a weird figure of stageland, especially in her later days, when her chief asset, her "voice of gold," was but a strange and feeble echo of its former strength, and when, maimed and incomplete, she masqueraded her age into youth, her femininity into the masculine, and her ugliness into beauty. Sarah at her best was a rich and interesting personality. She was a conglomeration of stage tricks with throat and hands, gesture, pose and diction. Her cheeks and ears were always grossly rouged. Her nails and lips were so coloured that it was no over-statement to compare them, as a famous critic once did, with a pillar-box. Her movements were sinuous, panther-like and undulating. They struck the horror that only fatal illness or excessive malevolence can awaken in the heart. Yet the terrifying beauty of the creature fascinated without chilling.

I saw Sarah for the first time over thirty years ago. She was so thin that she resembled the flat side of a rapier. She had the pallor of chalk, with two horrid roses of rouge splashed on her cheeks. Her part was the Lady of the Camelias, and the memory of her extraordinary voice, with its stabs and cooings of sound, its swaying rise and fall, its bursts and its ripples, is with me as I write. I looked upon her not as a woman—not as Camille, the woman of the play—but as some strange being from another world sent to show me what a marvellous instrument the human voice could be, how by the variations of its sound, and without an understanding of words, it could denote joy, suffering, ecstasy, doubt or fear.

Sarah had never the art of making you think. She could make you forget. She made you, by her art, forget her paint and powder, her artificial dropping of eyelid, her deliberate exposure of her teeth, her mechanical but triumphant smile. With her craft was paramount, sex assertive, and witchery ever present. As an actress she was never anything but herself, her wondrous, paralysing, self-glorifying self. Those who wish her well will welcome the end of her tragedy. For, to confess the terrible truth, it has come none too soon. Sarah lagged superfluous on the stage, and had become for the last few years of her life only a gorgeous but mutilated memory, a torso dream of the dead years.

XXXII

CRITICISM AND GREAT ACTING

I AM going to talk not only about criticism but about great acting. The stage is crying out for great acting. Our theatre needs it more than it needs great plays. Our dramas are indeed improving. During the last twelve months some remarkable productions have appeared, none of them strictly deserving the term " great " perhaps, but still, full of promise —full of brains—full of the sympathy and imagination that make for greatness. Too much nonsense has of late been talked about comradeship and the need for democracy in the theatre. Too many pleas have been made for a dead level of excellence in a company— for equality of artistic endeavour and fraternity of theatrical effort. Team work, of course, we must have. That is indispensable. But without the brilliant player no game is worth watching.

The great actor or actress has always been the mainstay of the stage.

When Shakespeare wrote " the play's the thing," he never meant us to lose sight of the fact that a great actor could make even " Titus Andronicus " a piece worth going to see. The electric spark of genius now so rarely seen upon our boards must be encouraged. There is far too much depreciation amongst us of the star system. That method of exploiting individual persons above others, above even the play, has its faults no doubt, but it also has its virtues. It calls for increased effort on the part of the performer. It impels him or her to give us of their best. It is the same incentive to an artist as the breath of a racehorse is in the nostrils of another. Vanity is an unpleasant trait, but even vanity has its value as a spur.

I have been told that by the severity and sarcasm of some of my criticisms I am discouraging ambitious and sensitive men and women from high effort. The truth is a good whip. Even critics need to feel its lash sometimes, and artists who are deterred by genuine, fearless, outspoken criticism from doing the utmost that is within them are not worthy of the name. If the criticism be just, it must be met; if it be unjust, it may confidently be disregarded. If it be mistaken, it may be ignored.

But the theatre for its future depends no more upon criticism, good or bad, than it depends upon any of the thousand and one other minor factors in the game. It depends primarily and lastly upon our capacity for producing great acting.

We have here in England as remarkable a body of players as exists anywhere in the world. For respectable, all-round excellence our directory of talent would be difficult to beat. But genius—that abnormal, amazing, and mysterious product of nature—where shall we look for it? The word genius is used over and over again in our newspapers as applied to modern acting, with what justification? Very little.

There was a time, and not so long ago, when geniuses did exist on the English stage—why not again?

Doubtless I shall be accused of reactionary principles for thus expecting and hoping for the re-advent of the Great Star. Phenomenal ability is in some people's eyes a simple expression of selfishness.   In mine it is the gold, the diamond, the precious thing we must all diligently search for.   We cannot all be stars, we cannot all be out of the common, but we can all do the best that we know how to do and strive with the whole of our souls.   The really great actor, when he comes, and he can only come after much striving of soul, will make everybody desert the cinema, the concert room, the debating hall, and even the eating-house.   People will stand for a whole day, endure untold tortures of discomfort in queues to watch his mimic passions and agonies, his whims and his grimaces.   Be he as diminutive as Little Robson, he will have the power to thrill you into ecstasies of admiration.   There are actors amongst us to-day—I must not mention their names— who stand at this moment on the border line of terrific achievement.   They are hovering— biding an opportunity—waiting patiently the time when play and part, hour and place shall coincide and unite in bringing them their rewards.   It is the critic's part to watch studiously these struggling, embryonic geniuses and help them in their upward climb.   To spare the rod of criticism may spoil the actor, to whom blame is as necessary as praise.

What are the essentials of great acting? Daring, originality, tremendous power in several directions, great range of passion and feeling, ·with the capacity for the quick, the sudden, the unexpected. Perfect control of the human machine in every detail and a personal magnetism that controls others, with unlimited painstaking patience. The definite purpose pursued to the end. Ability to characterise, to appreciate the humorous as well as the pathetic, the farcical equally with the tragic — the gifts of imagination, sympathy, insight, forethought, personal charm, and an equal grasp of the æsthetic as of the brutal. When one human being commands these things, or even a small portion of them, the attributes of divinity can be claimed. They are the qualities of genius.

Our training schools to-day are few in number, and such as exist do not present the same opportunities for practice of the art as existed in the olden days. It is not possible to create geniuses—they must come of their own accord —but by multiplying our theatrical schools and strengthening their resources, we are improving our chances of finding unusual gifts—strengthening undeveloped and latent histrionic power.

The stage has suffered greatly of late from indiscriminate flattery.   Every actor and actress, no matter what their true position, is hailed as a heaven-sent wonder or buttered with unreasonable praise as fulsome as it is untrue. Where a writer sees ability in a youngster, I believe it is his duty to stimulate with praise, and the warmest possible praise, the growth of that ability.   Where he detects or fancies that he sees mistakes on the part of either old or young, experienced or otherwise, it is also, I conceive, his duty remorselessly, relentlessly, yet fairly and scrupulously, to point out those errors, so that others may take heed thereby. What has the stage to learn from falsehood or even from critics who write " between the lines " ?   I go to the theatres and listen to certain critics in the intervals damning in no uncertain language certain performers for their mannerisms, their physical and mental shortcomings, and their private condemnations of these outrageous libels on God and Nature cannot be too forcible ; but I pick up the subsequent printed encomiums of the same individuals, and I am lost in astonishment at the gentle hypocrisy of their comments. They are charming humbugs, who disguise their dislikes and conceal their sufferings. It is this attitude of studied deceit—deliberate courtesy masking untruths with elegance of behaviour in print—that is going far to kill great acting altogether.

Some lady, angry with a criticism of mine, writing to me recently, referred me to Byron. Why, I cannot see, but I remember that it was strong criticism that spurred Byron from lassitude and ineffectiveness and brought him out of his puerile and piffling early versification into the strong and trenchant manly poetry which brought him fame and fortune.

After all, actors must remember that mediocre acting is like the mediocre in any other sphere of intellectual endeavour. Mediocrity is the shroud of Art. More good plays have been killed by mediocrity than have suffered through bad acting. The theatrical clubs are full of golf-playing loungers who are content to be " adequate," who prefer to play the " safe " game on the stage, to do nothing that will bring them into disrepute with their fellows, nothing

that will be " out of the picture." Courage
forms no part of their composition. Audacity
is the last thing they think of. Yet without
courage, without audacity, genius in acting is
impossible.

XXXIII

A VOICE FROM THE PAST

THE habit of indulging in reminiscences is not a modern one. They strewed rosemary in the year 1860 quite as well and as often as we do to-day. My friend Mr Gerald Maxwell, knowing a degraded habit I have of browsing upon theatrical literature of all sorts, has recently reminded me of that fact by generously despatching to my little library from his large one an assortment gift of surplus books, interesting links with the actors and theatres of the past, some amongst them dear old dog-eared and dingy volumes which have served not only to pass agreeably my spare midnights, but to bring forcibly home to me once more the eternal cycle of things. Nothing happens but has happened before. All has been said and said again.

Here is a little yellow cloth-covered thing, still fluttering and palpitating with life and

chatter, though the title on its back is inde-
cipherable with grime and its face is smeared
with ink and other blotches from the hand of
time—" Leaves from an Actor's Note-Book ; or
Anecdotes of the Green Room and Stage at Home
and Abroad. By George Vandenhoff. Edited,
with preface, by Henry Seymour Carleton.   Price
half a crown."   It is the sort of work that to-day
would be issued probably in sumptuous purple and
gold-covered boards, be priced at a guinea, and be
illustrated with photographs of all the fashionable
stage celebrities of the day.   Yet I would not
have it otherwise than it is.   It has the flowing
signature of a Mr " John Christie of Glasgow,
1862," sprawling proudly over its yellow fly-
leaf, showing that Scotsmen took as keen an
interest in the drama then as they do to-day.

Listen to the opening words of its preface.
They might have been written yesterday :—

" Despite the weak whinings of a certain class
of unhappy souls who are constantly growling
about the decline of the drama, and calling from
the mouldy past phantom ideals of actors and
acting as they should be, there is luckily a much
larger class always anxious for the welfare of
things theatrical ' at home and abroad.' "

The British drama was nearly dead in 1860. It has been dying ever since, and the lamentations for its end are perennial.

John M. Vandenhoff, the founder of the family from a theatrical standpoint, followed for nearly half a century the school of the Kembles. He was the father of George Vandenhoff, our author, whose interesting revelations of himself and his colleagues are just as full apparently of happy errors and unhappy truths as our modern pages of theatrical chit-chat in book form.

When I was younger than I am now it was fashionable amongst young actors to imitate the elder Irving, and I know of at least one promising tragedian whose career has been blighted by a slavish and ridiculous copying of the great man's methods, even to imitating his nasal and jerky delivery and his physical mannerisms. To-day it is the habit amongst some enthusiastic and clever youngsters to study Henry Ainley. " I pray you avoid it." " The test of genius (on the stage)," continues Vandenhoff, " is that it strikes out a novelty which it establishes as a truth—it creates a new truth, a new law. The great honours of the buskin have been won by men who earnestly devoted themselves to the study of their art, conscientiously and perseveringly mastering its principles." "Truth should be the artist's Egeria." "Edmund Kean's peculiar merit lay in his intensity, in his power of abstraction and of identifying himself with a passion—in his sudden transitions from the height of passionate expression to the familiar key of conversational earnestness." I could go on for hours quoting from this little book without, I think, boring anyone who was interested in the theatre. I will confine myself to Mr Vandenhoff's peroration.

"Let Press and public do its duty. The power is in their hands to sustain or to condemn. The amusements of a people take their tone from the people themselves, and the theatre is, of all institutions for the people, the one most subject to, most under the control of, public opinion."

Need I do more than humbly echo this exhortation ? Whatever is wrong with the theatre, Press and public have it in their power to alter.

XXXIV

TO THE UNPLAYED PLAYWRIGHT

It would be interesting to know the number of unplayed plays at present reposing in the drawers or cupboards of men noted or notorious in other walks of life than that of the professional dramatist. The critic has no need to say, " O that mine enemy had written a play ! " It is a thousand to one that he has—that is, if he be a man of brains or of any importance in the world of thought. If he has not written a play, you may be sure he has one written in his mind.

But there is no particular cleverness in writing a play. Any child can do it. The ability comes in in getting your play produced. Nor is it so difficult to sell your play to a manager, especially if you are a critic, a man of some renown, a personable fellow of attractive manner, or a journalist of influence and distinction. But when your play is sold, you will still have the difficulty of persuading the manager or manageress

who has bought it to produce it.   The purchaser
looks at the script, suggests alteration after
alteration, all of which you laboriously and
conscientiously undertake. He ruminates over
it for months, and even years, comes to the very
verge of putting it on—has all the costumes
ready, the scenes painted, the wigs fitted, and
then, presto ! another play comes along, some
actress departs from the company, a deterring
influence asserts itself, and your play is shelved,
never to be heard of again.

Every theatre manager's mood alters like the
wind. One day he fills the papers with para-
graphs about his intentions concerning you.
He will in the autumn produce Mr Fogg's
comedy, Mr Dogg's drama, and Mr Blogg's
farce. He has Shakespeare in mind and a
revival of old English comedy in view.
Euripides, Thomas Holcroft, and your humble
self all rub shoulders in the same puff preliminary.
But you all meet the same fate.   Exit all R.U.E.
Fame has played battledore and shuttlecock
with you in rehearsal only.   You retire dejected,
disheartened, disgruntled—down, if not out.

But there is with some managers a way of
intensifying the forces that make for actual

productions. Introduce capital or a capitalist, and the thought of lessened financial risk may at once rosily and favourably colour your chances. Faults will be seen with less severity —the readiness to criticise and condemn will not be so eager.

Yet here we have Mr Somerset Maugham, that most successful playwright whose success is due to the fact that his merits were first discovered by a private stage society endeavouring to encourage the tyro by informing him that it is far easier to sell a play to a manager to-day than it was when he began and when the public taste had centred upon and round a monopoly of Jones, Pinero, and Carton. Perhaps it is; I, personally, doubt it. The dearth of good plays remains apparently greater than ever it was. Our playhouses are reduced to reviving and reviving old favourites. The reason is that the risk of theatrical production, always temporarily high, has now exceeded all the bounds of sanity. It spells quick ruin to all but the completely triumphant.

The actor-manager took risks in the old days before the war; he couldn't afford to, but he took them because he was often an artist who put his work first and money-making second. To-day the commercial manager must consider money-making above everything else, because if he does not do so he will, with high rents, high salaries, costly orchestras, costly scenes, costly costumes, costly scene-shifters, etcetera, cease to be a manager at all.

The chief avenue that the unplayed playwright must seek would appear, therefore, to be the gloomy, narrow, uncertain, and unprofitable one of a scratch performance by a private play-producing society. Some of these societies have done admirable work in this respect, but they must redouble their activities and improve their resources far beyond the present limits because the plays that are clamouring to be produced are as innumerable as the sands on the seashore, and amongst them there may be, who knows ? a masterpiece or two.

XXXV

MACBETH AND PREDESTINATION

MY article on the above subject provoked the following interesting letter from Sir George Greenwood :

"That the witches are supposed to have been endowed with prophetic powers is certainly true, and inasmuch as prescience and free will cannot co-exist (except in some metaphysical sense known only to theologians), it is evident that, so far as their predictions were concerned, Macbeth was the victim of that constraining necessity which plays such a notable part in the old Greek tragedies. It was no doubt for that reason that Coleridge, as he tells us, was led ' to suspect our great dramatist to have been a studious Greek scholar.' Merely to say this, however, seems to me but a one-sided criticism. It leaves an important aspect of the play entirely out of sight.

"Mr Carroll writes : ' I judge Shakespeare

solely upon his plays as handed down to us. The rubbish that he was accustomed to throw in for their foundations may be dug up and sorted out by dustmen. I have no use for it.'

" I do not know if he would include Holinshed's history in ' the rubbish ' that Shakespeare so made use of, but I venture to say that no wise critic of the drama of Macbeth can omit to make reference to that old chronicle. Here he will read how, ' as Macbeth and Banquo journeyed towards Forres, where the King then lay . . . suddenly, in the midst of a laund, there met them three women in strange and wild apparel, resembling creatures of elder world, whom when they attentively beheld, wondering much at the sight, the first of them spake and said, " All hail, Macbeth ! thane of Glamis ! " (for he had lately entered into that dignity and office by the death of his father, Sinell). The second of them said, " Hail, Macbeth ! thane of Cawdor ! " But the third said, " All hail, Macbeth, that hereafter shalt be King of Scotland ! " '

" Further on we are told that ' this was reputed at the first but some vain fantastical illusion by Macbeth and Banquo . . . but afterwards the common opinion was that these women were either the weird sisters, that is (as ye would say), the goddesses of destiny, or else some nymphs or fairies, endued with knowledge of prophecy by their necromantical science, because everything came to pass as they had spoken. For shortly after, the thane of Cawdor being condemned at Forres of treason against the King committed, his lands, livings, and offices were given of the King's liberality to Macbeth.'

" 'The weird sisters!' An arresting title. The very name is suggestive of the mysterious, the uncanny, and the occult, and I believe that the majority of the readers of the play, and of those who witness it on the stage, imagine that it is a typically Shakespearean expression, and one which, perhaps, only the great dramatist could have conceived. Yet here we find it among 'the rubbish' that he threw in for the foundation of his great tragedy! And these 'three weird sisters' are 'the goddesses of destiny.' They are evidently the Fates—Clotho, Lachesis, and Atropos—in mediæval garb. So far, then, Mr Carroll is obviously right. Macbeth is an instrument in the hands of Fate; in some measure the victim of 'predestination.'

" But let us refer once more to Holinshed :
' The same night after, at supper, Banquo jested
with him, and said, " Now, Macbeth, thou hast
obtained those things which the two former
sisters prophesied ; there remaineth only for
thee to purchase that which the third said should
come to pass." Whereupon Macbeth, revolving
the thing in his mind, began even then to devise
how he might attain to the kingdom ; but yet
he thought with himself that he must tarry a
time, which should advance him thereto (by the
Divine Providence) as it had come to pass in his
former preferment.'

" Now here, surely, we have a glimpse of the
other side of the question. It had been prophesied that Macbeth should be thane of Cawdor,
and that prophecy had been fulfilled, naturally,
and without violence on his part, by reason of
the treason committed by the thane, whose
lands, title, and offices were thereupon given
him by the King. What, then, of the prophecy
that he should become King of Scotland ? He
might justly expect, and the chronicler tells us
he did at first expect, that this also would be
brought about in due course ' by the Divine
Providence.' The prediction was that he should

be King. It was no part of that prophecy that he should murder the then reigning King in order that he might usurp his throne.

" But we are told he became impatient because Duncan made his elder son Malcolm Prince of Cumberland, ' as it were thereby to appoint him his successor in the kingdom immediately after his decease,' whereupon ' he began to take counsel how he might usurp the kingdom by force,' and, further, ' The words of the three weird sisters also greatly encouraged him thereto, but specially his wife lay sore upon him to attempt the thing, as she was very ambitious, burning in unquenchable desire to bear the name of queen.'

" Here, then, is the other side of the picture. The witches — ' the goddesses of destiny '— have foreknowledge that Macbeth is destined to be King, and that Banquo's descendants are destined to be kings, but the dramatist leaves us free, just as the old chronicler does, to believe that Macbeth is not coerced by constraining necessity to murder Duncan, and to murder Banquo, and to attempt to murder Macduff, and actually to murder Macduff's wife and children. In short, Destiny in this drama plays a part far

short of that assumed by the *Ara*, or *Ate*, of
Æschylean tragedy, and the reader and the
audience are left free to condemn the ' dead
butcher and his fiend - like queen ' for their
bloody deeds. No moral Areopagus would, I
trow, acquit Macbeth in like manner as Orestes
was acquitted—as the victim of inexorable Fate.

" And though the weird sisters may be properly
described as ' goddesses of destiny,' the conception of them is very different from that of
the Moiræ of Greek or the Parcæ of Roman
mythology. The breed has become deteriorated
by an admixture of what Charles Lamb called
' the plain traditional old-woman witch of our
ancestors ' — a characteristic almost invariably
exaggerated on the stage—and they have become

> ' juggling fiends
> That palter with us in a double sense,
> That keep the word of promise to our ear
> And break it to our hope.'

" It was because he believed such promises
that Macbeth supposed it mattered not what
crimes he might commit, since he could not
be conquered till Birnam Wood should come
to Dunsinane, nor slain by any man of woman
born, both which things he looked upon as

impossibilities. But surely there is a difference between committing crimes owing to placing reliance upon the promises of a witch and committing them under the iron hand of Fate ! "

MY REPLY

My article headed " Macbeth and Predestination " has brought some interesting letters. Amongst them is one from Mr James K. Hackett, the American actor who recently appeared in the part with such success at the Aldwych. Mr Hackett tells me, amidst my blushes, that he has placed the excerpt in his Macbeth scrapbook " for future and authoritative reference."

He suggests that it might be interesting to start a discussion : " Was Macbeth a poet ? " It would be, he thinks, intensely amusing to see what arguments could be adduced by eminent critics, past and present, to prove the oft-repeated assertion that he was.

The even temper displayed by Sir George Greenwood is in pleasing contrast to that shown by the average Shakespearean controversialist, who generally seems to consider the most trivial difference from his own fixed opinions as an outrage upon himself and an affront to the god of his idolatry. I hasten to assure Sir George that I had no idea whatever of " throwing a new light " upon the character of Macbeth. In response to two correspondents who evidently wished to burst the soap bubbles of their own foolish ideas upon the ceiling of Shakespeare's fame, I tried to explain and elaborate my notion of a Macbeth depicted by the dramatist as a creature driven by higher powers to a fate it was useless for him to try and avoid. I claim no originality for this thesis. Far better minds and abler pens than mine have explored and dissertated upon it and found in it much to agree with. If it is not a correct view of Macbeth I am in very good company in my error.

I cannot, whatever Sir George Greenwood or anyone else may think of me, consent to the interpretation of Shakespeare through the medium of or with the help of Holinshed. That respectable chronicler (like Herodotus and so many other celebrated historians) was no better than an inspired liar. The fact that he was not conscious of lying does not affect the result.

Moreover, Holinshed was revised, expurgated, and edited to death. His text, as we see it to-day, is probably as undependable as that of Macbeth, and the very passages that excite Sir George Greenwood's interest and admiration may have been written, not by Holinshed, but by John Hooker, *alias* Vowell, an able and scholarly editor of the historian, or by the printer of the work, under whose direction the histories were written.

Plays must surely be judged, not upon the histories their authors have utilised or the reference books they have consulted, but upon the text, and the text alone.

I agree cordially with Sir George Greenwood that there is a difference between committing crimes through reliance upon the promises of a witch and their commission under the iron hand of Fate, but I hold that difference to be one only of degree. The very reliance in question may be part of the machinery of fate. In the old Greek drama Destiny used all sorts of factors for its ends: The breaking of the Witches' word of promise was deliberate, and not accidental. That circumstance is to my mind sufficient to make the Witches' actions part of the web of fate spun around Macbeth, that web in whose meshes he finds himself so fatally involved.

I refer all readers interested to Professor Richard G. Moulton's "Ancient Classical Drama," and particularly to his chapter on "Macbeth Arranged as an Ancient Tragedy." No one has better explained my own standpoint. "Its action," he writes of Macbeth, "rests upon the same oracular mysteries which the Attic tragedians loved, and the same spirit of irony underlies the movement of its story." This remark, coming from a man who knows Greek tragedy backwards, is surely very strong testimony.

XXXVI

RECONSTRUCTION FOR THE THEATRE

" My dear fellow—the theatre—what is it ? A mere place of amusement—a very necessary form of public recreation, no doubt, but lacking the importance and significance you attribute to it—quite unworthy the attention of a statesman except from the ' bread and circuses ' standpoint." That is the opinion of the average politician and the opinion also of the average Englishman.

And the cause of the theatre is too often belittled by those whose duty it is to uphold it. The dignity of the actor's calling was always present to the mind of the late Sir Henry Irving. It has been loyally and consistently sustained by Sir Squire Bancroft ; and to-day we see evidences amongst the younger generation of players — chiefly the despised actor-managers and actress-manageresses — of a desire to sustain their profession as well as to be sustained by it. Not from entirely selfish motives does Miss Marie Löhr produce such a work as "L'Aiglon" nor Mr Robert Loraine become Cyrano de Bergerac.

But what has Mr Henry Arthur Jones to say about the theatre of to-day :—

"Under the protection and with the passport of the Lord Chamberlain, *the sodden vulgarities and imbecilities of our established form of national drama grow bolder and bolder, and occasionally blossom into flagrant indecency.* . . . Thus the game is played, with *rosy twaddle, flaming licentiousness and crude sensation* always at the wickets, while common sense and sanity are warned off the field by those who take the gate-money."

I have taken these words from the foreword to a little work on "The Reconstruction of the Theatre," written by Mr G. E. Morrison, the President of the Critics' Circle. They seem to me to draw a lurid vituperative and extravagant picture of our stage ; but then Mr Jones was ever given to occasional over-emphasis. Like Collier, he blows the horn vigorously in order to be heard. If this is the sort of thing said about the theatre by those who love it—

those who are its apostles and stalwarts—in what sort of respect can it be held by those who despise it, or by those who know nothing of and care nothing for its claims ? If its friends abuse it, what can its enemies not say ? " Save us from our friends " is no answer. The indictment may be highly coloured, but it has a basis ; the fire is there, hence the smoke.

Mr Morrison, the author of this pamphlet, to which Mr Jones has contributed these condemnatory opinions, is a dramatic critic whose ability it would be an impertinence to question. His erudition, his analytical power, his Scottish air of aloofness and impartial superiority, his fearlessness and bluntness, tempered with a scrupulous sense of fairness, make his criticisms enjoyable even to those who suffer by them. He is one of the very few writers on theatrical matters whose views may be read with eager and respectful interest, even when they differ from our own. Not without fearfulness and bated breath do I therefore venture to join issue with him on some of his conclusions and recommendations.

I know someone worse than the Demagogue. He is the Bureaucrat. Ever insolent of office,

to get at him you must fill up three forms, follow
the attendant, go down or up three flights of
stairs, enter two lifts, take the corridor to the
right and the sixth door on the left. Then he
will refer you to another circumlocution office
infested by another animal of the same variety.
I loathe the London County Council. I abhor
the Lord Chamberlain. But not even Mr
Morrison and the whole of the Critics' Circle
in conclave will persuade me that Messrs Dilly
and Dally, masked by Comedy and Tragedy,
will make better substitutes as controllers of
our stage, and they seem to be Mr Morrison's
only remedy for the evils caused by lack of
effective theatrical supervision. He wants to
bring about a new and special department, a
single authority with no business than the
theatre that shall use a single form of licence.

There is a lot to be said in favour of
his arguments. The facts he adduces are undeniable. I am sceptical only of his remedy.
I do not believe in the control that is too
evident. Children are better led, better per-
suaded than forced—and these children who
play on their passions for us, whose mimic
existences convert us ourselves into children,

blotting out our sorrows and worldly cares, must not be made too sensible of stern authority. Rough treatment makes delicate plants die. The flower of art must be handled gently. Emotion that has to keep one eye on the County Council inspector and the other on the Lord Chamberlain is as worthless as the smile of the wanton with one eye on the policeman.

The formation of a trade union for actors and actresses is again considered a sign or symptom of the desire for theatrical reconstruction. But the Boilermakers' Society will not permit a discharged officer to enter their ranks until he has in their opinion been properly trained to their " skilled craft." Have the actors such a rule ?

" The theatre of to-day," says Mr Morrison, " demands the undivided care of an authority with all the will and the wit and the power necessary to cure it of its present distempers." He wants a proper unified control of the theatre to take the place of the present divided jurisdiction. I cannot conceive of any authority short of God capable of a real cure.

With the thought that it is high time the theatre was taken in hand sternly, I sympathise.

But I think the matter rests not with outsiders, with onlookers, with the critics, or with officials, but with the players themselves and with the playgoers. The manager easily can be put in his place if the public decide to dislike him or his methods. No amount of severity on the part of officialdom will reconstruct the theatre. It may cleanse and purge it, but sweeping a room is not building a house—and here there is a temple in ruins, not a broken dog kennel to be repaired. It is the reconstruction of the national conscience that is at stake. The theatre is the gatehouse of the soul. Mr Morrison is concerning himself with the bailiffs.

Surely the truth is that neither Capital nor Labour, as politically understood, have any real part to play in the development and fruition of dramatic genius, which after all is the copingstone of the theatres. To reconstruct the theatre we must revive its priesthood. We must convert it from a shop into " a place where God is." Where the hush of reverence and fast attention betokens the presence of a Great Spirit. The actor who respects his art and himself will make himself as envied as Ion was of Socrates. " He is no rhapsodist who does not understand the whole scope and intention of the poet, and is not capable of interpreting it to his audience."

It is not control we require so much in the theatre as the sense of real freedom. Real reconstruction can only come from the natural growth of creative effort, spontaneous initiative. The subordination of the conventional to the true and beautiful would be the principal aim. Enthusiasm—foolish, joyous, unrestrained—that is what we most need to properly reconstruct the theatre. Absolute devotion to their art on the part of actors—pride in its possibilities. Unlimited contempt for those who pander and betray. Without these no reconstruction is possible.

XXXVII

AUDIENCES

ARE you, who read this idle scribbling upon an idle business invented for idle people by the still idler, one of our new audiences? If so you must forgive me for speaking to you after my custom, frankly and openly.

Why have you not as yet learnt how to behave yourself in the theatre? Has it ever occurred to you that the first theatre was something in the nature of a church?

It was with growing astonishment and concern that I watched your conduct at a playhouse the other evening. I am speaking to you, Miss New Playgoer, whose acquaintance with old-fashioned manners and habits is obviously limited. You were accompanied by an amorous old bald-pate, and neither he nor you had the slightest consideration for the poor devil seated in front of you who had paid fourteen shillings for the privilege of sitting in a stall to see and hear the entertainment. For what reason your companion and yourself went to the theatre on that evening I cannot think.

But you were not alone in your bad behaviour. The stalls seemed full of folk who, like yourself, were not in a mood for theatre-going and who only wanted to chatter and gaze rapturously at each other. The only decent-mannered people, apart from a few isolated strange and curious specimens, were in the cheaper parts. Civility, sobriety and quiet seemed to have transferred themselves to the pit or the upper circle. As for you, my dear young creature, you had not begun to understand the first principles of play-going. Your conversations were animated, shrill and incessant. You touched upon every topic from " If Winter Comes " to the last time you were at Murray's Club. You referred to the Academy and the portrait of Lady Rocksavage and " the appalling lack of imagination shown by these modern artists." Your gabble rang in my ears for the best part of the three acts. You wore beautiful silk stockings and Regent Street shoes, and you displayed a feverish anxiety to exhibit the shapeliness of your legs, for you stuck them upon every possible opportunity on an empty stall by my side, swaying the seat up and down when you did so, possibly out of a pretty and infantile love of motion. It was probably for the same reason that your companion prodded me incessantly in the back with his knees and coughed every now and again down the back of my neck, but the temporary annoyance caused by these little happenings was an emollient compared to the effect upon me of your running fire of criminally senseless observations made upon the unfortunate actors and actresses doing their best for you upon the stage.

That bright little monthly the *Curtain* has just been counting up the number of coughs, sneezes and throat clearings at one of the most lavishly draughty of London theatres. It appears that its representative counted 249 coughs, 318 throat clearings and 12 sneezes during the first act alone. He counted in all 2967 throat sounds from the audience. Five hundred and sixty-two genuine hard coughs (the kind meant to be heard), 748 smothered explosions of the kind that cannot be suppressed, 692 genteel, deprecating coughs, 162 coughs where the cougher tried to pretend that it was not really a cough at all but only a little burst of sound. I did not hear you cough. Your other noises made coughing superfluous.

I remember that when " John Bull's Other Island " was played at the Kingsway, Mr Bernard Shaw issued a printed notice in the programme requesting the audience not to interrupt the performance by laughing too much at his jokes, or applauding any of the sentiments given expression to by the characters. I remember also that Laurence Irving in my presence once " told off " an audience at the Garrick Theatre for what he considered was rude behaviour. Yet these pre-war audiences had the politeness of the Chinese compared to some of our modern-day monstrous collection of profiteers and newly-rich outsiders. How often have we to sit next to ladies who seem to be carrying on their persons all the most suffocating perfumes of Arabia, or rub shoulders with asthmatical old wheezers who go to sleep and make strangely stertorous noises during the play with their mouths open intermittently and erratically and without any sense of dependability.

Of course, I know what these dear people will retort upon me, Why aren't the plays more interesting? Why am not I as a critic more interested in them? If the actors were better, they will say, I wouldn't notice such trifles as prods from my next-door neighbour's elbow or the puffing of peppermint in my face, the crunching of silver paper from chocolates, and the clatter of teacups during the performance at matinées. I really can't say if there is any justice in such an answer, but I do feel that when audiences behave themselves both actors and play take on different values. There is a remarkable difference in the same play seen with a different audience. A play that is given in the afternoon, though it may have the same title, the same cast, the same plot, and the same dialogue, is never the same play when it is performed to an evening audience. Audiences are never alike for two nights running. They never laugh at the same points or take up the same applause for the same passages. An audience in the provinces makes a play seem quite different from the same piece when it is acted in town. A piece played in one part of the provinces is a different piece when it is enacted in another part. "Bunty Pulls the Strings" is a different play in Torquay, Glasgow and London every time. And so is every other play, be it tragedy, comedy, drama or farce.

I hate smoking in theatres, *i.e.* in what is so strangely called the legitimate theatre. It would be a catastrophe, to my mind, to watch such a delicate fantasy as " Dear Brutus " through a haze of somebody else's tobacco smoke. I should not mind it so much through my own or through Barrie's.

The discomfort usually attached to the seating accommodation has a lot to do with the restlessness and inattention of audiences. Bad plays may be made endurable by comfortable seats. The faults of a good play are aggravated by having to dodge a pillar or a huge piece of head-wear or by the knowledge that any minute your seat may give way and precipitate you upon the floor. In one of the best of London theatres I have seen a whole row of stalls collapse. In another I have myself been suddenly flung forward, crushing some priceless Parisian creation upon its fair wearer's head. How can audiences be expected to behave under such conditions ? When Shaw paid his first visit to a theatre he was much more interested in the audience than in the piece, and as some

plays go nowadays, it is far more amusing for a
critic to turn round and contemplate the actions
of his neighbours than to try and discover what
the actors are talking about. After all, in con-
formity with the canons of etiquette, is it not
worth while to try and live up to the pretence of
decent play-going ? If we cannot vitally interest
ourselves in the drama, should we not try to
respect the desire for peace of those who can ?
An occasional yawn is pardonable, a titter in
the wrong place is perhaps excusable, but a
prolonged and persistent disregard of everybody
else's comfort in a theatre has never been
regarded, except by a few of the best circles in
Modern Society, as indicating gentility.

My friend Mr Turner, of the Grossmith and
Malone management, once told me about a
gentleman who demanded from him a top price
seat in a flood of Billingsgate directed at the
box office, and who was exceedingly annoyed
because there were no guinea stalls for him to
sit in, whilst, by his appearance and conduct,
he would have disgraced the pit. Shall we ever
attain to the dignity of the one-price theatre ?

My heart is really too full to deal adequately
with this topic. If ever I become a rich man,

rich enough to run a daily newspaper on the
drama, I shall have a theatre entirely to myself,
where I shall be the sole spectator, and no
one else shall be allowed to disturb my placid
and entire enjoyment of the play. It shall be
played for my sole and especial benefit, and no
one shall be allowed in besides myself, not even
the dramatic critics.

XXXVIII

" ROMEO AND JULIET "

SOME INVITATIONS TO ARGUMENT

BENEATH the most beautiful human form clanks a skeleton. Behind the loveliest face grins a skull. Underlying the romance of " Romeo and Juliet," if you strip away the lyrical charm, the rapturous passion, and the wondrous verbal beauty, you will find as ridiculous a story as ever came out of Italy. Whoever wishes to be satisfied as to the wondrous extent of Shakespeare's genius has only to analyse this play. The dramatist has adopted an absurd tale of immature love, wholesale murder, and double suicide, and converted it by poetical wizardry into the most popular and passionate of the world's love tales.

The average playgoer's idea of Juliet is that she was a charming young woman of about eighteen or twenty who had the misfortune to fall in love with a handsome young fellow named Romeo, belonging to a family in mortal enmity with her own. He has a vague idea that these "star-crossed lovers," by misunderstanding and through a meddling Friar, were led into separately committing suicide, and that " never was a story of more woe than this of Juliet and her Romeo." But how many people realise that the real Juliet was only thirteen years old ? According to Lady Capulet, of a " pretty age." They were certainly forward young ladies in Verona, for at an even younger period ladies, according to the same authority, were already made mothers. Lady Capulet herself was a mother at the age of twelve. Making every allowance for the eager Italian temperament, this precocity seems to put to the blush the flappers of the Strand.

How many people have realised that the very first words Romeo utters to Juliet upon seeing her for the first time in her father's ballroom are an invitation to kiss, and that he has not spoken five more lines of the text before he *has* kissed her. To put it shortly— he meets her on Sunday, marries her on Monday, parts from her on Tuesday, and dies with her on Thursday.

No dramatist from America, the land of hustle, could conceive a tragedy of such speed or a heroine of more rapidity than this. How few spectators of the acted tragedy and how still fewer readers of the text ever appreciate these facts?

Such is the intoxicating, bewildering beauty of the poet's workmanship that we are never sensible for one moment of the impossible crudities upon which his tragedy has been constructed. Listening to his music you can only think of the sweetness of the rose, the languour of the nightingale's song, the softness of the southern spring. You drink the purest wine of pleasure, you feel your heart beating with healthy passion, the blood of youth comes back into your crinkled veins, and you thank God for a genius who can tell you a love story free from sentiment and sickliness, and inspire your middle age with the wild throb of youth.

Consider Juliet's inquiry as to whether Romeo is a married man, and her comical insistence upon his honourable intentions. What modern novelist or playwright would dare to conceive a heroine of this stamp? In these degenerate days we have heroines who refuse to have marriage conferred upon them in order that they may be made so-called " honest " women, and before long no doubt we shall come to the point when a heroine will appear who will refuse to be satisfied with anything but a married man. But with mediæval drama we must take Juliet's nice concern for her moral security as one of the necessary qualifications for a lady of quality. Her passion is not equal to brushing aside the conventionalities.

No one can fail to admire the lyrical marvels, the rhythmical juggling with words, the exquisite play of fancy in this play, and as instances of mediæval love poetry the various scenes with the lovers are unsurpassable.

As Hazlitt has pointed out, it is the only tragedy written by Shakespeare entirely upon a love story. I do not at all agree with the same authority that Romeo is simply Hamlet in love. He seems to me quite a distinct personage in his disposition as well as his actions. Romeo, if one rudely subjects him to analysis, is almost as foolish a person as the love-sick Orsino in " Twelfth Night." The love affair with Rosaline makes him cut such a contemptible figure. A gentleman who sheds tears and

" adds to the clouds more clouds by his deep
sighs," who shuts up his window and locks the
daylight out, making himself artificial night
merely because a lady will have nothing to do
with him, yet a few days afterwards falls
violently in love with the first pretty girl he
meets, can hardly have much strength of
character.

But in this, as in everything else, the glamour
of the words makes us lose sight of Romeo's
folly, and we think of him only as a handsome
fellow whose leg excels all men's, and with
whom Juliet could not help falling madly in
love the moment she saw him.

The Italians of every period have been fond
of these stories of amorous and bloody intrigue,
but as told by Shakespeare this particular
tragedy becomes a marvel of harmony. We
listen to the flood of music and sit enchanted,
and we do not know which to admire the
most, the delicacy, the purity, the gentleness,
the sad sorrow, or the tragic grandeur of the
composition.

It is a play that is seldom acted to the critics'
complete satisfaction. Charles Lamb contended
that the love dialogues were sullied and turned

from their nature by being exposed to a large assembly. When the discerning ones are satisfied with the Juliet they generally find fault with the Romeo, and I have even known them come out of the theatre praising nobody but the Friar Lawrence. The literary qualities of the play lend themselves to mouthing and conventionalism, and it is seldom one finds a Juliet worth listening to until she is old enough as an actress to play the nurse. Romeo is too frequently a mere walking-stick for the Juliet.

The chief difficulties managers who produce Shakespeare contend with are their own utter ignorance of Shakespeare's intentions, and the performers' wilful ignoring of the obvious meaning of his lines. Only occasionally do we find a producer with a proper understanding and a firm grasp of the essential points of the plays. One man will give you Shakespeare overloaded with scenery and expensive costumes, another will in the opposite extreme produce him on bare boards with black curtains. Freakishness, extravagance, or ineptitude seem inevitable with nine out of every ten Shakespearean productions. Mr Fagan's middle method, seen recently, has consequently proved refreshing and novel. The real beauty, harmony and poetry of Shakespeare seem in general to be the last things aimed at.

The task confronting an actress who essays the part of Juliet is not exceptionally difficult, though it demands considerable talent. Much of the character plays itself, as they say, in the profession. Romeo I consider a far more difficult undertaking. Both characters call for an overwhelming flood of passion, an irresistible capacity for melody, and, above all, for the charm of youth expressed through the mind of maturity.

XXXIX

THE PLAY OF THE FUTURE

I RETURN to this question of the drama of the future with reluctance and diffidence. Still, I have a few conjectures and one idea which may be worth transcription. I fancy I can detect looming out of this wilderness of revues, musical plays, etc., certain healthier tendencies. I seem to see a more vigorous theatre. One with greater virility, with no use for problems of the meticulous and nasty. A theatre that will discard all " slice of life " theories, and the ill-concealed cynicism, suggestiveness and sordidness of certain pre-war pieces, a theatre that will prefer wholesome, strong-blooded yet brainy drama. A play which will, as Wordsworth said of the ideal epitaph, " speak in tones which shall sink into the heart." I smell amongst our future dramatists " Fe-Fo-Fi-Fum, the blood of an Englishman."

Now for the idea. It is an old idea of mine,

probably not new to others, one which theatrical managers who know their business so much better than I can teach them will probably pronounce impracticable, crazy. But it may lead to something.

I have always held that London needs at least one theatre solely for experiment. A theatre where pieces can be tried, where authors can be produced and actors and actresses tested—in short, an experimental professional playhouse. A combination of experienced producers, acknowledged artists, and proved dramatic authors, with a leavening of the untried and unproved. That such a theatre could, if properly run, be a great boon not only to the play-going public but to actors and theatrical managers is, I think, self-evident.

The greatest drawback to the theatre is its costliness. You cannot experiment on the stage under our present system unless you are a millionaire or a lunatic. That is why I ask for the theatre of experiment.

I am fully sensible of the entertainment value of many present-day plays. I quite agree that in their way some of them are brilliantly clever and far wittier and more intelligent than some ambitious, serious productions. But is there not, I ask, a big public waiting for *the real play*? And is not the precentage of theatres at which *real plays* can be seen unfairly small in proportion to the number óf theatres available for frivolous, amusing musical pieces? If we can by co-operation evolve an experimental theatre we might solve satisfactorily the whole question of the future of the drama.

There is an association of theatrical managements. There is also an actors' association. I humbly suggest that it might be possible for these people to combine. Let each management subscribe a certain sum per year towards the cost of such a theatre. Let the actors agree to assist on sharing terms in running it. Let the united theatrical organisations elect annually their own theatrical director, the various theatres contribute from their respective stores all the scenery, dresses and properties required for each production, taking it in turn, perhaps, to supply the building for the plays selected by the committee for experimental production. All new plays produced could be the joint property of the co-operative corporation, and successes could be sold for the benefit of all concerned by tender to the highest bidder amongst the managements participating.

As for the class of play to be tried out, opportunity should be given for every sort of piece—the tragic, the serious, the poetic, the comical, the whimsical, the fantastic, the spectacular. There should be revivals of all the famous old plays, the classical plays, and the pieces which are milestones in the history of the drama, and actors and actresses desirous of testing their mettle in certain classic parts could have an opportunity of doing so at no expense to themselves, and with a possibility of financial profit. For five days in the week old plays could be revived, the sixth given over to the production of the new piece.

I have thrown out this idea scrappily and hurriedly, but it is worthy of elaboration.

XL

ON TRAGEDY

A PLEA FOR ITS REVIVAL

ARE all our theatre managers afraid of tragedy? Do they think that the world tragedy through which we have passed so recently has created a dominant call for lighter fare, a demand so eternal, so insistent, so selfish, so all-consuming that tragedy must keep in its dressing-room for ever, or bury itself in the Green Room for good? Is the scarcity of the tragic element in the theatre due to the fact that we have so few actors and actresses capable of tragic impulse? Have our dramatists no new tragedies in their lockers? Whatever the reason, the fact remains that high tragedy is at a discount in the English theatre to-day. It is a pity. The great tragedy is a noble thing. It must have moral truth as its foundation. It must be profoundly, persuasively ethical. It should teach us how to govern our lives. It assists us in control of ourselves. It calls for simplicity in design—simplicity in treatment, sublimity of theme, and courage in facing the inevitable. It has to be of a finer texture— cast in a purer mould than any other form of dramatic composition. It is the only form of play in which Grandeur has any place. It is the only medium through which terror can be terrible, despair desperate, and beauty beautiful. It is the only real vehicle for stage eloquence. The English language is not only at its happiest, but in its most elevated mood in tragedy. The greatest passions become ignoble, pitiful or laughable, if passed through the mint of any other kind of drama. With the aid of the truly tragic writer they take on rich lines and wondrous forms that dignify them and idealise them beyond our dreams.

There are some playwrights who love to snarl at the heels of humanity. Others spend their lives transforming life into ultra-sympathetic and sentimental toshery. These men cannot think tragically. They will never be the mighty spirits of the theatre. They do not, or will not, see mankind whole. Many writers can compose stage poems, but not tragedies. The solemn ruins of civilisation are not for them. They try to make a tragedy of feelings that prove a comedy to all who can think. Is there such a thing as Destiny? There are happenings that make us think so, and it is these events that make for tragedy. The sanguinary melodrama is as far removed from pure tragedy as farce. True tragedy needs a stateliness of style, a chaste severity of word painting, an appeal to the imagination that drama of the melodramatic order never approaches. Horror of itself does not make tragedy. The workings of fate—the tricks of chance—the sport of the gods—these factors provide material which your author, skilled in tragedy, can fashion as he will. We must suspect the lofty abstraction that passes for tragedy. We despise the tragedy that has no joy, no humour, no wisdom in its soul, but only gloom and fear.

The real objection to tragedy is that it so often verges upon prosiness, and tedium and dullness is the unforgiveable sin in the theatre. The structure of few tragedies will bear analysis. The best of the skeletons upon which our poets have laid such wonderful flesh, grin and leer at us in their sheer frightfulness. Looked at in the bone, they would not survive being thought of. The greatest tragedies are those that will not bear contemplation and at which everyone laughs.

But as a matter of political and social welfare let us restore Tragedy to her proper place. We need no bombast. No furious thundering, clamour, and no anguish unsupportable but a realisation of the thought " In the Great Hand of God I Stand." Let us not be daunted by the thought that Lear is unactable, and that Pepys thought " Romeo and Juliet " the worst play he ever witnessed. The callow critic may sit in his stall sucking a pencil stump over a silly farce. He cannot do his calling justice until Madame Tragedy holds the stage. The cult of virtue is a peculiarly English vice. It cannot be practised in a finer, higher or more efficient way than in pursuit of the tragic muse.

XLI

THE CURTAIN

IS IT ESSENTIAL?

ART movements have the same degree of permanence in the theatre as elsewhere. They have no more. Each new idea commences as a protest against its forerunner, and ends protesting against the idea that takes its place. It does not surprise me, therefore, to find Mr William Archer—one of our most noted writers upon matters theatrical—a critic formerly remarkable for the advanced and progressive attitude of his mind and for his breadth of outlook, now in his later stages assuming the air of a bored octogenarian thoroughly contented to let things remain as they are, sublimely contemptuous of any and all attempts to improve or substitute fresh means for those various mechanical devices by which it is sought to create stage illusion and surround the actor.

From where I write I am not so far away
from Salzkammergut as Mr Archer appears to
be, yet even here I find the same obstructional
and reactionary sneer employed by reigning
" authorities " to denote contempt for what is
styled the non-theatrical theatre. But when is
a theatre not a theatre ? And when is it
a theatre ? Does the mere possession of a
proscenium and a curtain constitute a real
theatre ? Is the present mode of theatre
construction indispensable to dramatic art ? Is
not intensely interesting drama creatable from
three actors and a wooden plank ?

Mr Archer says that the curtain is essential.
He suggests there is something invincible in
the " mystery " of the proscenium cloth. The
mind that can adopt so primitive a conclusion
has abandoned all consideration of either art
or amusement. It has surrendered to habit,
and the older we grow the more confirmed we
become, as a rule, in the belief that our oldest
habits are the best.

Mr Archer is characteristically superior to
the attempt made by many modern theatrical
producers at " mixing " audiences and actors.
Why, however, may one ask, should they not

upon occasion be " mixed," or, to use a better because accurate term, be blended ? At its best as well as at its worst the playhouse is a temple of convention. When we come to accept as a convention the practice of stationing certain players amongst the audiences it will be as rational and as conclusive as the convention by which after every act one curtain descends or two curtains close.

I have seen in Brussels, at a performance of " A Man's Shadow " in French, the witnesses drawn from the auditorium instead of from the stage itself, and the dramatic effect was far more stimulating so far as I was concerned. It made me feel as if I were an actual participant in the dramatic action. The Forum scene in " Julius Cæsar " played in the Grosseschauspielhaus at Berlin gained tremendously for me by the shouts and cries that came from every part of that huge house. In Moscow, I am told, the audience are actually enlisted as part of the play, and are given their cues just like ordinary actors. All this may seem supremely ridiculous and destructive of illusion to Mr Archer, but it is in this direction the modern theatre is tending.

The present form of theatre has grave dis-
advantages, and the future must and will
overcome them. I cannot understand anyone
praising our existing methods as the last word
in theatre construction. They have the handicap of presenting a picture in the flat instead
of in the round. The playhouse of to-day is a
two-sided or a three-sided experiment in both
optics and acoustics. Whatever Mr Archer
may say to the contrary, there is no special
magic in the curtain.

The intelligent use of light can create a far
better effect and bring about far more satisfactory results than those possible with cloth.
It can cause that effect in an infinitely more
mysterious, awe-inspiring and illusion-creating
manner. You can with the aid of light and
darkness illuminate or shut out a scene either
gradually or suddenly, and with a black-out
you can drop a curtain that will not suffer from
stoppages during its descent, and with strange
bogglings and disturbances that destroy all that
has gone before.

Whilst we may admit that the present form
of stage has given us much, let us not forget
what it has cost us—and what we have lost by

reason of it.   Has there been no loss in oratorical
or elocutionary value ?   It may be argued that
the theatre has no use for either oratory or
elocution, and that in any case we have out-
grown the need for both of these ancient gifts.

But what is the chief curse of the English
stage to-day ?   The fact that one can so seldom
hear from it pure English clearly spoken.   The
stage must teach us once more how to speak
our own tongue.   We are growing careless,
slipshod, slovenly with our tongue, our lips,
our teeth.   We neglect the beauties and charms
of English well spoken.   Go and hear Sir
Johnston Forbes-Robertson speak Shakespeare
and you will understand how much, how very
much, this means.   The platform stage that
projected into the audience had the virtue of
inciting if not compelling a rounder, clearer
and more definite method of enunciation.   There
is now not one theatre in London where consistently one can hear English undefiled.   Words
are run into each other.   Ends of words are
slurred.   Slang and lisping jostle each other
for supremacy.

It must not be supposed by Mr Archer and
his adherents that those of us who see in the

proscenium arch or picture frame stage a source of danger or unhappiness in result have any fixed resolve to suggest a return to the ludicrous shortcomings of either Greek or Elizabethan theatres. We see that the present stage is but a first step in theatre craft, that we have as far to go as the scientist had before the discovery of wireless. The future conceals boundless possibilities where the theatre is concerned. Stage architecture is not taken with sufficient seriousness.

Mr Archer says that " the obliteration of the frontier between the mimic and the real world is not only detestable but nonsensical." These are strong words and as impeachable as such verbal extravagances generally are. For what is it that constitutes and defines the frontier between the imaginary and the real? Is it Mr Archer's much-loved curtain? Is it the proscenium? or the well of the orchestra? It is none of these things. Whatever frontier exists in the theatre of to-day is a preciously little one, it is constantly being transgressed by the players and the dramatist, and it is made solely by the minds of the spectators themselves. It can just as easily be limited by the railing between the pit and the stalls as by the footlights. We read a book, but the frontiers of our imagination are not enclosed within its covers. We study a painting, but the thoughts it inspires are not circumscribed by the frame.

It is staggering to see such an acutely penetrative and analytical mind as that of Mr Archer's confusing the material employed with the objective of dramatic art.

Humanity has always been, and will always be, superior to stone and wood in the theatre as well as outside it. We may be pardoned for loving our old toys, especially when we are grown up, but we must not let our toys dominate us and delude us into a belief as to their indispensability. We are in a playhouse, and its toys have an irresistible love of change. The venturesome, the experimental, the inquiring student of the drama will have an ever-open mind in age as well as youth.

Mr Archer describes the stage of to-day as a final term in a long process of evolution. Has anything more absurd been written? Who can talk of finality with safety? The magic of the theatre, its irresistible wizardry, depends upon the genius of the dramatist, upon the genius of the actors, and upon the hearts and minds of the playgoers. It has but the smallest dependence upon the material means employed to house them. Three players and a passion make one forget all the splendours of St Peter's at Rome.

XLII

FRENCH ACTING

THE POLICY OF PERFECT ORAL DELIVERY

I HAD a particularly enjoyable experience recently in watching on a Sunday afternoon a performance, at the Comédie Française, of Corneille's tragedy, "Horace." In this form of "classical" drama the French actor is generally seen at his best. Again and again I have advocated the necessity of utilising in this country our theatres, or at least a reasonable proportion of them, for the furtherance of the cause of English speech. There is no better method of learning how to speak a language than to listen to that language accurately delivered, and there is no more effective means of exhibiting the virtues and difficulties of a language than through the medium of experienced, cultivated and expert actors. The French stage has many vices and weaknesses, but it has the supreme virtue of recognising the necessities of the French language and its claim to proper consideration from those who are privileged to use it. Slovenly pronunciation is as absent from the Comédie Française as that pedantic and artificial insistence on accuracy sometimes insisted upon in certain German theatres. The malacostomous player has no place within its walls.

At this particular performance the audience had the privilege of listening to classical drama, spoken with perfect rhythm, perfect expression, studied beauty of cadence combined with an assumption of sincerity of feeling and passion. It is comparatively easy for an actor who knows his business to exhibit symptoms of anger or indignation, love or hatred, but it is supremely difficult to combine a correct exposition of those feelings with a poetic and unimpeachable utterance.

I have never been an admirer of that slavish adherence to tradition that too often disfigures and handicaps the performances of the Comédie Française, but I respect and revere unreservedly that portion of their inheritance that teaches them to respect the magic of the French language properly and correctly spoken.

Now, what is possible to these French artists is certainly not impossible for us. Our schools of acting are paying, no doubt, a great deal of attention to this aspect of the histrionic art. Producers and those who direct our theatres generally must also, at the risk of being criticised for pedantry, abolish from their stages these bad habits in elocution and enunciation that make lovers of pure English writhe in their seats and deprive the occupants of the gallery from the right of understanding what the players are saying. Even in the cheaper and more popular theatres in Paris, where melodrama of the broadest kind is played, the actors are always audible and reasonably accurate. In modern French comedy, while a certain rapidity is inevitable, the speed at which the play is taken never causes a great sacrifice in the matter of distinctness.

As to the matter of most modern French plays I prefer to say little. The few new comedies I have seen recently concerned themselves, as usual, with sexual problems, with all those delightful improprieties which only the French know how to render innocuous. Most of the horrors of the Grand Guignol the last time I

was there were either stale or tepid, but the
season had not opened, and I was not fortunate
enough to discover any special novelty.

I was greatly interested to read the other
day a comment by a French visitor to England
upon the sentimentalism of English acting and
English plays. He pointed out that the same
play performed in England and in France
received in the former country a treatment
of sentimental glamour, false and sickly, and
opposed to the true spirit of the idea which,
interpreted in France, received that degree of
cynical levity and witty irony without which
the play had no artistic justification. No one
could possibly accuse the French stage of to-day
of being lachrymose.   It is as hard, as polished
and as brilliant as any diamond. Unfortunately,
its sparkle too often rests upon the heaving
bosom of easy virtue. There is no cynicism,
of course, in Corneille's " Horace." It is inevitably a tragedy, and in high tragedy there
is little room for the cynic. The work of the
average modern Frenchman, on the other hand
—M. Louis Verneuil, for instance—is nothing
but cynicism from start to finish.

XLIII

BRUTUS AND BARRIE

Men at some time are masters of their fates.
The fault, dear Brutus, is not in our stars, but in
ourselves that we are underlings.

FROM these words spoken by Cassius to his
friend Brutus, Sir James Barrie has allowed the
sprite of his imagination to weave one of the
quaintest, most amusing and delightful of stage
fantasies.

The lines themselves falsify their implication.
For where would Brutus have been had there
been no Cassius ?   But it is not to Shakespeare's
" Julius Cæsar " that we must look for the
true source of this prank of the imagination.   It sprang from " A Midsummer Night's
Dream."   " Dear Brutus " is a variant on that
wonderful Shakespearean blend of coarse matter
and fine fancy.   It is a modern inspiration,
springing from restless thoughts of Robin
Goodfellow, of an enchanted wood, of a mid-

summer night, and some " might-have-beens "
of humanity.

It is a veritable lobscouse of a play, a mixture
of petty crime, human weakness, fairylike
fantasy and fragrance ; in its light parts it has
something of the ironic quality of Gilbert's
" Engaged," yet there is nothing mordacious
in its humour, merely a genially penetrating
satiric quality.

The " lob of spirits " is replaced by a real
Lob, an active old practical joker, in his nonage,
who coaxes and pets the flowers in his garden
until they simply have to grow up. His bald
and wrinkled front looms up from the darkness
of the night, his ferrety nut-brown eyes leer
under senile lids pendulous and saggy. Lob
dotes upon pulling chairs away just at the
moment elderly ladies propose to sit down
upon them. He has a singular trick when
seated of projecting his leg into the air rigid
and premonitory. He crawls under the table
and cries like a child when he cannot get
his own way. He has the gift of disappearing
and reappearing suddenly. He passes through
the play contemplative, alternately *méchant* or
benevolent, boding good or ill according to his

mood, an elderly, neatly groomed, Dickensian gentleman, sallow faced, long fingered, alertly reposeful, the imp grown up.

Lob as host has, in his country house, a thief, a drunkard, an idler, a would-be adulterer and his wife, a sterile woman, a proud lady, and a philandering girl. This oddly assorted crowd has one thing in common—all desire a second chance in life. Lob himself is a small part of the play, which is mainly one of lost loves. With such an author as Barrie, one can only listen sympathetically and intently when lost love is the theme. You will find in the story no love of the conventional stage pattern. There is the lost love of a drunken husband for the memory of an adorable untamed thing, a bluntly beautiful goddess, the love of his youth echoing feebly in the woman who is now his wife. There is the lost love of that wife for the once gay and generous young artist who wooed and won her from the chase of other men. Best of all there is the lost love of an imaginary father for an imaginary daughter. "Lightly, musically made, so light upon the grass," a dream child, the thought of whom brings the unhappy pair back to happiness.

And there are other lost loves in the piece, but they are of no importance compared to this one.

There is the lost love of a philanderer that is no love at all, merely a passing of the time. There is the lost love of the proud lady Caroline Laney, a disdainful lisper attracted by a thieving butler. Hers is a slavish love that hides itself under a mask of scorn and contempt. But what are any of these loves against that affecting picture of imaginary fatherhood doting on daughterhood divine. The woodland full of barky elm and shady oak, the dewy glade, the eglantine, the cowslip and wild thyme, the hawthorn brake—what are any of these charms against the magical beauty of parent and child seeking art and nature simultaneously in nature's heart.

If the play is a tragedy of the lost love it is a comedy of the second chance. How many of us at this moment are sighing for a second chance in our lives, and what good would come of it? What would be the result to us if that second chance came? Some of us are unchangeable. As it is said in the play, there are three things that never come back to man—the spoken word, the past life, the neglected opportunity.

Nothing is said, however, of the unspoken word, the future, or the opportunity seized and regretted.

This play establishes, if it establishes anything, not that the fault is in ourselves that we are underlings, but that some things are written in the stars. It was fated that Margaret should be a dream child. " Of all sad words of tongue or pen, the saddest are these—it might have been."

The wild anguish of that despairing cry wrung from the dream child left in the darkness alone in the wood—" I don't want to be a might-have-been "—must pierce the heart through and through of every childless mother who hears it. It is one of the most cruel yet most exquisitely moving moments in modern stage fantasy.

What a midsummer madness the play is ! None of the folk are real. Each is a child of whim. The night of adventures and misadventures in the magic wood that springs up in a night and disappears with the morning leaves some of the venturers into it just as they were. Others it changes strangely. Yet we accept all inconsistencies and dubieties and

never ask for explanation. The recollection of
that enchanting scene in the wood between
father and daughter—that scene so full of joy,
so full of sadness, so full of humour, pity, pain
and tenderness, blots out all blemishes of craft
and kills the critical furor in the most captious.
Has there ever been a more poignant, heart-
rending moment on the English stage than
when this poor sodden wreck of an artist is
made to realise that this beautiful daughter
exists only in his dreams? He cries out,
" When I was in the wood with Margaret,"
and can get no further. He repeats these
words, and again with slower, deadlier tone,
till we can almost hear his heart break. His
glorious daughter is for him worse than dead—
she has never existed.

A dramatic triumph this, of the highest kind,
for author and actor.

Yes! Your American who travels thousands
of miles to England to hear the nightingale in
the New Forest should go instead to Wyndham's.
He must take no notice of the mechanical
whistler, that shirt-sleeved and perky fellow
who stands in the wings and reminds us of
Hans Andersen and his Chinese warbler. Let

him listen instead to Philomel, the bird of
nature, the bird of Merrie England, of Puck
and of Barrie. He can wander deliciously in
Lob's Wood, and, if so disposed, dispense with
the lady of the nut-brown eyes or with the girl
who is " so fluid." He may be inclined to jeer
at the piping of the elderly Pan in the forest,
his jigs and his reels, but when he lights upon
Margaret and her father he will draw something
good out of the lucky-bag and hear a real
songster sing at last.

And now just a clumsy attempt to recall
Du Maurier-Dearth. I bracket the names
together, for I cannot decide where one begins
and the other ends. It is of no consequence,
for both men fascinate me. Æsthetic to his
finger-tips, looking as if he had just stepped
out of the Latin Quartier, yet, as Lady Caroline
would say, " viwile," his hair just streaked or
flecked with grey, broad browed, big headed,
high cheek-boned, two great lines dimpling
themselves around the mouth to the chin, with
a one-sided smile on his compressed lips, this
marked, snub-nosed personality towers through
every scene in which he appears. Note
the Dearth of the first act, with his flushed,

bibulous face, his dissolute underlip, his haggard
defiance of society, his round-shouldered abandon.
Here is the devout undertaker for decanters.
" Crack o' my eye, Tommy ! " How he can
put the port away !

See with what a wealth of ingenious yet
natural and entertaining " business " the actor
decorates and relieves his lines. His easy play
of body. The shrug of shoulder, the swing of
arm. Can any other player manipulate so
variously and continuously a cigar or a match ?
All his many mannerisms are arresting. See
with what an abundance of felicitous gesture
and movement he marks the character, how
gracefully he leans against the back of a chair,
passes his hand round the back of his neck,
or places his knees against the table with
Bohemian ease. With what decision he can
rap his knuckles on the table to emphasise a
point ! Note, then, the Dearth of the wood,
the swift humour of this other fellow-self,
his slouching, devil-may-care liberty, his fond
playfulness. Here is contrast indeed. The
abstemious, industrious, vigorous searcher after
truth and beauty, with easel, palette, paint
and brushes. One knows that when he shouts

" Daughters are the thing " he means every word of it, and that it comes from the bottom of his heart. And how he slaps and pummels that daughter in lovable parental domination ! He takes her by the throat one moment, smacks her softly across the mouth ; the next he may seize her whimsically by the ear or throw her away from him and pull her towards him. He buffets and banters her so that it becomes almost a game of human bat and ball—a teasing monster, a devoted bully.

And in the final act his distant peering into the past happiness of the wood, into the might have been, his yearning, his sentiment, his anguish, his hopefulness, the amazing variety of his moods complete a performance that can only make us proud of him, proud of the English stage. It is acting of quality, that no comedian, English or Continental, can approach for restraint, dignity and delicacy. It is a clear-cut, tenderly beautiful creation.

We appear to be discovering, rather late in the day, that nearly all of Barrie's plays bear revival. What a poor, unsatisfactory word it is—" revival." Why do we apply it to plays that have never died ?

XLIV

THE FUTURE OF THE THEATRE

It is time to think of the future of the theatre. National reconstruction problems are beginning to face us on every side in all their grim immensity. And there is no more tempting field for the reconstructive enthusiast than the dramatic stage.

But can the theatre be reconstructed? Is it worth while?

The acting profession is the only one that obstinately refuses to take itself seriously. It is a remarkable mixture of vanity and modesty; of overweening egotism and lack of self-respect. Now and again we find a man like the late Sir Henry Irving holding an exalted and dignified view of his calling, and continually doing his utmost to sustain the public respect for it. But how often is the actor content to regard himself very much as the court jester, a public clown ready to gyrate like a monkey, wear his heart on his sleeve, and sacrifice all his finer feelings for some five or ten pounds a week and a few empty rounds of applause from the unthinking!

In this country we have the finest actors in the world. Hurl your brickbats at me. I repeat it. No other country can show such a large number of talented actors and actresses—people of education, gifted with true histrionic instinct, full of good-fellowship for each other, reasonable in their ambitions, blessed with high spirits and confidence in the future. But what are we doing with this mass of talent and hopefulness? Little or nothing. We drive our ablest performers into the music hall, into revue, into musical comedy, into farce, into any form of entertainment short of their legitimate business—that of acting.

Can we reconstruct the theatre upon a sound acting foundation? Is it desirable to do so? We can institute a Government Department to foster the growth of cabbages and potatoes. We can busy ourselves over the position of the village pump. But when it comes to stimulating the imaginations of the people and awakening their moral impulses and their intellects through the medium of the stage, we differ and dally and do nothing.

Never was there a greater need for a National Theatre than now. Never was there apparently so little hope of its realisation. Yet with the true perversity of circumstance now is the time to expect the unexpected. With the return of millions of men into civil life from the black theatre of war, the stage on which they have faced the tremendous issues of death and self-sacrifice, upon which the heroic has become the commonplace, a great change must inevitably take place in both our theatre and its audiences. It is interesting to speculate what form that change will take and into what channel the after-war actor will direct his energies. It is hard to believe that there will not be some greatly imagined ambitious attempt on the part of our battle-stained youngsters to attack the problems of the theatre with virility and brains. The theatre of the future must gain tremendously in vitality, if not in finish, from our soldiering. We may see an added interest in spectacle. Productions on a gigantic scale in melodrama and Shakespeare may be expected. The general discipline of the theatre may be improved.

The vexed question of personalities *v.* representation on the stage will not be solved by the establishment of democratic ideals, because even in a democracy personality must always count. But there will be more and better schools of acting and more opportunities for serious students of the theatre. At least I think so.

The public will never cease to regard the theatre as a vehicle for amusement, a recreation, or an anodyne. In war-time such a state of affairs is not only pardonable, but essential. But after the war those of us who love the theatre, who have humbly tried to plumb its potentialities, must see to it that the theatre occupies its proper intellectual pre-eminent position amongst the arts we respect and practise. If we fail to make as much progress in the world of the theatre as we must do on the path of science, we shall be unworthy our heritage.

XLV

THE MARIONETTE PLAYERS

THE melancholy caused in me by the Italian puppet show was profound and complete. I cannot conceive anything more calculated to destroy the self-respect and esteem of human beings than this damnable dancing and nodding of dolls. For, alas! they are as human as we are. They betray the same ambitions, the same affections, the same little vanities. They strut with the same unwarranted pomposity or cringe with the same unjustifiable air of humiliation or protesting weakness. And they are so sure, so steadfast. What action is there of ours that these wretched little things cannot execute with infinitely greater audacity and decision than we can? In many points they excel us. They can defy Time. They can scorn Temptation. If the Gods made them a happy face it remains so till the end. They have no sense of evil. In their worst moments they can point to the wires by which they are pulled and demonstrate absolutely their own innocence and absence from complicity in any crime.

It is so tragical—at least, I found it so—to be made into a child once more and to be put, as it were, again into your nursery with your toy players and your miniature theatre.

It made me realise and review all the strings by which my own life has been pulled this way and that from childhood. It made me see that had I not been such a puppet, responsive to the pullings of others, I might not now be cavorting so comically and with such futility in these later years upon my human pins. The puppetry of life ! The life of puppetry ! What is there to choose between them—at least, for ordinary men ?

Behind these scenes, too ! What an absence of professional rivalries and jealousies is here ! How indifferent is each performer to others' failures or success. Here is no private sniggering at each other's deficiencies—no envy, no backbiting. How self-contented and how free from all those pinpricks that drive some living players frantic are the marionettes. Imagine the feelings of a theatre manager who can

rest on Fridays without a constant demand
for increases in his salary list, who will never
be faced by obstreperous and temperamental
puppets refusing to play the parts assigned to
them or to speak the author's lines. Here are
no private vices or diversions from duty to be
feared. Every evening each little wooden actor
comes with the same gay readiness to do its
duty, and should a failure to the play result
there will be no black looks or gloomy faces.
These little folk will be as constant, as cheerful, and as impenetrably philosophical as ever.
Hisses will fall upon them unheard.

XLVI

SHAKESPEARE'S VERSE

LIBERTY FOR THE ACTOR

VEHEMENT protests have recently been made against what is termed the " slovenly " delivery of blank verse said to be noticeable in Shakespearean performances amongst modern players. The term " slovenly " is a misdescription, and constitutes a libel upon those conscientious, if misguided, actors whose intentions and labours deserve a greater consideration than such an epithet bestows upon them.

Certain precious theorists, more distinguished for a pseudo-æstheticism and literary dilettantism than for their knowledge of theatrical requirements and the actor's art, are asserting, without the slightest justification for doing so, that Shakespeare's verse must necessarily always be delivered as verse, and not as, what it undoubtedly is, verbal material for an actor to use to the best advantage of poetic drama. I do not say, in answer to them, that every element in Shakespeare must be sacrificed to a regard for the illusion of life, but I do say that the main object of drama is to be poetically and dramatically natural, and not necessarily poetically and æsthetically unnatural in order to comply with convention. To borrow a Shakespearean expression, the actor must, even in verse, blank or rhyme, always "hold the mirror up to nature."

This desire for the "naturalistic" on Shakespeare's part, as well as on that of many modern intellectual interpreters of Shakespeare, is described by these literary pedants on pedestals as an error. Possibly from their "æsthetic" point of view it may be, but the question that the public have to decide, and which they have already decided in no uncertain fashion, is which of the two methods is theatrically right. The principal object in the delivery of Shakespearean blank verse must surely be to see that it is not "blank" in two senses of the word. A full appreciation of syllabic and metric perfection, a sense of rhythm, balance, stress,

and scansion are, of course, desirable qualities in
the actor, but they must not be emphasised at
the expense of dramatic feeling and the instinct
of true imaginative insight.

Shakespeare wrote his plays solely for the
stage. He had not the slightest idea when he
was writing them that they would in future
ages be subjected to all this searching examina-
tion by academic rushlight from literary experts.
I have the greatest possible respect and admiration for literature as literature in its proper
place, but some of the finest plays I have seen
have been written by people who knew nothing
of literature and cared less. Some of the worst
have been composed by men whose pre-eminence
in literature was undoubted. We go to a theatre
for the play and the acting, not to listen to
recitations of blank verse.

Because I argue that the verse of Shakespeare
must be subordinated to the dramatic sense of
the lines I am accused of wishing to destroy
and deface Shakespeare's poetry, but it will be
found that Shakespeare himself provides the
key to the actor by breaking up his own
blank verse wherever passion, thought or impulse seems to call for disturbance of his lines.

Marking the verse in a verse-play must not be a matter of rigid pedagogic rule, otherwise there will inevitably be loss of dramatic vitality, no matter what may be said to the contrary by people who have never been compelled to practise the art of speaking blank verse themselves to see how much passion and feeling they can get into it tied down by poetic cords and regulations.

By all means let us have all the poetry possible in Shakespeare, but if we allow actors to work upon the plan that Shakespeare was poet first and dramatist afterwards, we reverse the natural order of things, upset the principles that Shakespeare himself has laid down for our guidance, and run the risk of lessening the public interest in Shakespeare, which has fortunately been restored and renewed by the vitality, vigour and natural force of such productions as we have recently seen at the Court and St James's Theatres. Here the poetry is brought out sufficiently and the dramatic purpose always paramount.

There is no excuse for " gabbling " Shakespeare, and there is no excuse for not extracting as much music out of the lines as the words themselves and the situations call for. But, on the other hand, a too stilted regard for the music and measure of the lines purely from a poet's point of view is going to the other extreme. The solution of this problem lies, as in most things, in balance. The actor must have a proper regard for his medium, but must not allow his method of speaking blank verse as verse to kill Shakespeare's matter. Shakespeare trampled on blank verse whenever it suited him to do so, and the actor of genius will follow his example.

XLVII

SOME NOTES ON ACTING

CONTINENTAL AND ENGLISH

ALTHOUGH the " odorousness " of comparisons is notorious, I shall endeavour to set a contrast between English, French and German acting. I should say that English actors are easily first in the general finish and average polish of their performances. In pure comedy they excel both French and German. There is a taste, a discrimination, a nice regard for balance and perspective, and the finer qualities of a study in English acting of the better class than can ever be found in either Paris or Berlin. The humour is more delicate and refined, the power of suggestion greater, the cut and thrust more dexterous and neater, the passion more skilfully retained. But where are our tragedians? Where even our melodramatic actors to-day ?

The war seems to have effectually stifled

tragedy, and the tragic actor for the moment, so far as England is concerned. It is not so in Germany. The power, the intensity, the sincerity of the German actor and actress are undeniable. But with all their force, there is a coarseness—a cumbrous, ponderous, elephantine viscousness that clouds the horizon and deadens the vision. In their comic passages they are just as clumsy. Vulgarity too often asserts itself with stentorian voice, and banality has its followers in farce just as with us.

The French artist, on the other hand, is never awkward nor pompous. He is often insufferably egoistic, irritatingly confident, cocksure and buoyant, but he has the manner of the actor, and plays always lightly and easily. There are actresses in England who overflow with emotional instincts, but do not know how to control for theatrical purposes the streams and torrents they let loose upon their audiences. Your Continental actress can seldom be accused of this fault. Neither German nor French woman, however free of expression she may be, ever loses that final curb which enables her to make the great effect of sudden breaks and full stops to cataracts of passion. George

Henry Lewes was very fond of referring to what he termed the ground-swell of emotion. By this he meant the rebounding yet gradually subsiding waves of feeling striking upon thought. It is in picturing the ground-swell of anger where the Continental actress is so admirable.

Of course, every actor depends so much upon his listeners that the character of audiences must inevitably be considered in reflecting and comparing the capacity of a player in a particular country. There is no audience in the world so responsive as an English audience, so eager to enjoy itself, so ready to accept what is given to it in the right spirit. The German audience is intensely critical, silent and apparently devoid of approbatory functions, yet one can feel in its tense stillness and attentive quiet the reality of its appreciation for that which is good.

The French audiences are also very critical, but more demonstrative than the German. They are, upon the whole, much better behaved than English audiences, the members of which often disgrace themselves by speaking loudly during the play, clapping in the wrong place, shifting uneasily in their seats, and laughing at the wrong moments. The better an audience behaves the easier it is for actors to act, and whilst one would hardly wish to go so far as Bernard Shaw and forbid all laughter during the show of a comedy, it is not asking too much that people should preserve a greater dignity and avoid the loud laugh that speaks too often the vacant mind.

I have seen German actresses who for dignity, impressiveness, charm and talent compared more than favourably with any French or English women, and the capacity of the German companies for playing unselfishly together was a never-ending source of wonderment to me. In the French theatres I found as a rule each performer more anxious to score individual points than to register points made by others for the benefit generally of the play. Miss Mary Nash the other day told me of an amusing label that was attached by an American critic to a certain actor. He was described as having a cue-face. This meant that his face only lighted up when his own cue came. A prevalent fault this with many English actors.

The chief fault I have to find with English acting is its persistent recognition of audiences.

But, bad as our own actors are in this respect, they are much less annoying than the French, who seem deliberately to engage the people in the front of the footlights in a language of the eyes, and to solicit at every possible convenience their approval and encouragement. I am never tired of inveighing against this artificial habit, which destroys whatever little sense of illusion the theatre has had left to it by the monkey tricks of producers who do not know the simple alphabet of their profession. German players undoubtedly score over both French and English in this respect, inasmuch as they always appear to be quite oblivious of anything but the scene in which they are engaged.

Their movements are natural, and arise out of the necessities of the action, and are never introduced superfluously or for the purpose of " breaking up " dialogue, as is so often done here. Whilst we can undoubtedly teach both French and Germans a great deal, it is equally true that we have a lot to learn from them, and if only we could assimilate some of their sincerity and earnestness to add to our delightful sense of comedy it would be all to the good.

XLVIII

DU MAURIER AS ACTOR

AGAIN and again I hear it said that Gerald
Du Maurier is a bad actor. " Pooh! My dear
chap—a delightfully charming personality, full
of his own mannerisms ; a graceful, easy,
polished, cynical individual of marked type,
who can always be relied upon to play himself
into your interest and affections, a man who
is always the same. An actor ? No ! ' Gerald '
cannot suppress himself and become someone
else—can never think with another man's brain
nor feel with another man's feelings—nor adopt
his outlook on life, his walk, his gestures, his
vitals. He mumbles his words and is always
drawing his finger across his nose or the back
of his head." Of some such sentence, less
long-winded perhaps, but equally emphatic,
might my friend, " the authority," deliver
himself with oracular, familiar, and final
damnatory sniff. And at times I confess I

am tempted to listen and assent. But not always.

England has no finer player than her Gerald Du Maurier when he likes to act. He gives you such pleasure in so many ways. He is always acting pleasant people pleasantly. He has to. For the public will have their favourites in pleasant parts. But I have seen him—in " The Ware Case," for instance—play a rather unpleasant person with arresting and terrible power.

Observe that, with insular and narrow conceit, I am claiming him for England, ignoring his French origin, name, and persistent Gallic levity. Before I explain why, let me try to examine with some particularity his acting in " The Prude's Fall," running with great success since the first week of September last year at Wyndham's, despite considerable adverse criticism of play and actor.

It was not my fortune, good or bad, to see the first performance. I was on the Continent at the time studying the modern Frenchman in the flesh. So this latest English stage picture of a Frenchman in England escaped me until last Thursday evening.

Doubtless you know the story of the play. Let me jog your memory. The gallant French explorer-adventurer and aviator, Captain Andre Le Briquet, goes to the little English cathedral town of Norman Arches (note the Norman—a nice touch) to renew acquaintance with the charming Englishwoman—Mrs Audley—whom he met first at Assouan. He has his first favourable impressions of her spoiled by her prudish refusal to receive socially another casual friend of his, Mrs Westonry, a lady who has loved unwisely and too well. He thereupon deliberately proves to Mrs Audley, through his own person, that " passion " (which he calls " love ") is liable to come to any woman at any time, and overthrow reason and every other consideration. Thus does he teach her the virtue of toleration. It is not a wholly pleasant or credible tale, but it has its acting qualities, and I need concern myself with it only as illustrating my opinion of Du Maurier as a fine " *actor* " in the proper accurate sense of that word.

In the first place, his " Le Briquet " is French, clearly, unmistakably, definitely. He speaks English very well, and his lapses into his native

tongue are commendably few—too few for
verisimilitude in fact. But his appearance, his
colour, his attitudes, his accent, his vitality,
volatility and volubility, his sensuousness, his
critical, cynical, semi-contemptuous mixture of
passion, egoism and humour are French of the
French. He makes love as only a Frenchman
can or would. He talks French as well as
it has ever been talked, even on the French
stage. Whoever says otherwise can never have
truly observed or listened. I do not think the
authors have helped him in the character.
They seem to me to have drawn a very bad
Englishman masquerading as a very good
Frenchman. For instance, would any French
gentleman ever behave with such extraordinary
lack of fine feeling, or treat with such want
of true chivalry an Englishwoman of so refined
and sensitive a nature—Mrs Audley? But
having to behave like a cad and a blackguard
both from a French standpoint as well as an
English one, the actor, with consummate skill,
lightness, and delicacy, yet full-bloodedness,
glides through scenes that, with a less accomplished player, would assuredly repel to the
last degree of nausea.

This fellow, stripped of his Du Maurier veneer, might make us echo Dr Johnson and say: " What can you expect from fellows that eat frogs ? " Or, again, to transpose the French poet, De Belloy, make one say : " The more I see of foreigners, the more I love my own countrymen." With the actor's art antipathy vanishes. We pardon all—astonishing, but true.

This particular study of Du Maurier's interested me as much as anything I have seen him do, and I remember him in the old days at the Comedy and His Majesty's long before he joined in management with Frank Curzon, or before he discovered " Raffles."

He is a master of the game of expression by suggestion. A solitary look of his spells volumes. He devotes himself to the scene, and never " fixes his eye on some man in the pit and sings at him till he laughs," a favourite method with many comedians since Harley's day. He has a cat-like dignity, a kitten's playfulness. At times he is given to rapidity, a modern failing which leads to indistinctness of utterance, but which adds to the naturalness of his impersonation.

To be natural is his first consideration. His quickness at a point and his certainty with it when seized are equally notable. He is not an actor of sudden and violent contrasts, and can consequently never be greatly successful in tragic or serious passages. His variety, however, wants for nothing, and he can move from grave to gay, from lively to severe with the facility of a Wyndham.

His voice is not powerful, but it is penetrating and capable of interesting differences. Though he has obviously studied in the French school, his acting art is essentially English. All his methods are English. The repression, the quiet finish, the slyly comic good-humoured restraint of the man mark him as English, despite his French ancestry.

To say that he has succeeded on his personality may be correct. But to say that he is not an actor, as the critical understand acting, is a libel. He can " act " as well as anyone when he has to.

XLIX

" THE PROMPTER "

It is not enough to speak, but to speak true.

A FAVOURITE recitation commences with the words, " I remember, I remember." Someone must compose a new poem for actors entitled " I forget." And this brings me to a little note of warning. Too many times of late has the prompter's voice been heard on first nights. Why is this? He ought not to be heard at all. The prompter must be banished from our theatres, or he will empty them.

It is, of course, notorious that some of our finest actors and actresses have bad memories, that they suffer from first-night nervousness, that " fluffiness," as it is called, or hesitation is one of the rights of the distinguished. But nothing makes an audience more restive, nothing sends an author into more awful fits of depression than an obvious ignorance of his text on the part of the players. I often think that the prompter's box should be placed with us as it is in France in the centre of the footlights. The necessity that sometimes arises of shouting right across the stage to some nervous and forgetful performer ought never to happen. It has been suggested to me that payment for rehearsals has something to do with this insecurity and uncertainty on the words. If it is so, and I should be very sorry to believe it, it is a disgraceful state of things. The actor to be a true artist must place nothing in front of his work, not even remuneration. The manager to be worthy of his responsibility must not allow small pecuniary considerations to stand in the way of his own success and that of his company. Sometimes uneasiness in the script comes with over-rehearsal. We must state the happy mean. And, again, prompters are prone at times to be too prompt, too ready to give the word before it is wanted. The ideal prompter is a treasure.

L

GOOD-BYE

IT has occurred to me that some of the readers
of this book may be curious to know my reasons
for surrendering the responsibilities of dramatic
criticism. This is what I wrote when giving up
my position as dramatic representative of the
Sunday Times :—

" I leave the *Sunday Times* and my work of
dramatic criticism for its pages of my own free
will. I (and doubtless many others) hope that the
cessation will be permanent. I have completed
exactly five years of association with a newspaper that has in its time boasted of such men
as Clement Scott, Joseph Knight, Herman Klein,
Malcolm Salaman, the first Lord Burnham, J. T.
Grein, and many other writers of repute as its
dramatic representatives. I have devoted to
theatrical journalism on this paper one year more
than sufficed Bernard Shaw on the *Saturday
Review*, the periodical that Mr Agate my successor
has hitherto represented. My resignation has been

so frequently tendered to the proprietors of the
Sunday Times that, though they have not grown
tired of refusing it, nor, strange to say, tired of
offering to increase my salary, they realise that I
am tired of offering to retire and must actually
carry out my intention now if I am not to do so
later on under the orders of a mental specialist.

I retire with mixed feelings of bewilderment
and pride. I feel like a man who has at last
succeeded in breaking a bad habit. I feel that
I have finally conquered a deplorable weakness
of my character, but it staggers me to find I have
succeeded. I think of the plays I have tried
to damn and the huge fortunes they have made
for their perpetrators. I think of the struggling
actors and actresses I have scorned, and how, in
spite of my jeers and sneers, they have reached
the topmost rung of their profession. I think of
the managers whose work I have derided, and I
watch them rapidly paying off their vast arrears
of past indebtedness, and I murmur to myself
humbly and dejectedly, ' Quo Vadis ? ' I think
of the wonderful old gentlemen who, after years
and years of constant playgoing and theatrical
penmanship, still preserve a miraculous serenity
of outlook, a clearness of vision, and the saving

grace of humour, in spite of the obvious futility of their efforts. And I fall exhausted into an easy chair, or is it on a sofa ?

The truth is that, although I love the theatre insanely, passionately, and in a wholesale and indiscriminate way every aspect of its ever-changing and intriguing features, I cannot any longer love her as a wife—I must treat my hobby as a mistress, a secret love, a private attachment, as I did in the days of my youth and early manhood. I was never a constant wooer. I can endure all sorts of slights, all kinds of caprices, the other excitements and even the damnably dull periods of courtship, but I cannot be chained to my beloved, except with chains of my own forging. I cannot go on with dreadful reiteration every Sunday proclaiming to the housetops my temporary boredoms and the innermost flutterings of my affections. Not all the notes in the *Sunday Times* treasury will tempt me to do so.

So I have only to thank my readers for their patience and good nature. They have astonished me. What I have done it has amused me to do. I hope it has not been without amusement for others."